100% Confidence

Why Direct Sales/ Network Marketing is booming again and what it means for you.

Ed Ludbrook

"The future belongs to those who see possibilities before they become obvious"

John Sculley, ex-CEO PepsiCo and Apple Computers

"Confidence is the bridge connecting expectations and performance, investment and results.
It underlies the performance of individuals, teams, businesses, schools, economies and nations."

Rosabeth Moss Kantor

The exciting thing about an industry evolving is that it creates new opportunities for the individuals and companies smart enough to look to the future rather than the past. If **you gain the vision, you gain the confidence** to act when others are not. To create extra-ordinary wealth when others do not.

Evolution is the natural way of things. Understand how it works and be empowered and inspired by it.

Network Marketing is evolving in the most fundamental way in its history. Whilst the developments driving the evolution seem small, their impact is dramatic because they create a business which appeals to the Intrapreneurs in society.

When the same situation happened in the Franchising industry it created a growth boom that is still going strong 20 years later.

What would you do if you
knew you could not fail?

Def: **Intrapreneurship**

*'is the practice of entrepreneurial skills
and approaches within a company or at home.'*

Wikipedia

Entrepreneurs are the life-force of business today. They are the risk-takers who exploit opportunities to start and grow businesses pioneering new products, markets and business strategies.

Whilst many dream of rewards of being an entrepreneur, few are prepared to take the risks necessary to succeed as an entrepreneur. This is why most people are Intrapreneurs.

An Intrapreneur exploits opportunities yet within the security of an established organisation, thus the term 'intra-entrepreneur'. Whilst potential rewards are lower than starting your own new venture, the risks are significantly reduced so the possibility of success is dramatically increased. It is a compromise that the Intrapreneur are happy to make.

The Employee Intrapreneur who uses entrepreneurial skills to exploit new opportunities for the organisation. They are not common.

The largest quantity of Intrapeneurs work for themselves yet in cooperatives, networks and the franchise industry. They gain the freedom of owning their own business yet also wants the security of a proven business working within a large corporate support organisation. They make up the vast majority of business opportunity seekers.

If any industry can offer the best Intrapreneur opportunity they will drive that industry. The best example is when franchising changed and a flood of Intrapreneurs have driven that business for twenty years.

The new developments in Network Marketing means it now offers the ultimate Intrapreneurial Opportunity.

Also by Edward Ludbrook

The **Big Picture** [replaced by Shakeout! then 100% Confidence]

Tidalwave

International Networking

The Network Coach

The Fundamentals of Network Marketing

Great News – 12 months of articles from London's Evening Standard newspaper

Nature's Own People

Nutraboom - the future of the Health Product Industry

How to Coach

How to have a Fantastic Year in Network Marketing

100% Motivation

100% Success Basics

100% Success Coach

100% Leadership

Introduction

I remember so clearly the day when a friend suggested I look at a new business he had joined. He did not try to explain it to me, just encouraged me to attend a presentation to be held in a church hall next to the Houses of Parliament, Central London. I attended and listened to the presentation on a new form of 'low cost franchising' called Network Marketing and it was the most exciting concept I had ever heard.

That night, the presenters claimed that Network Marketing was 'the future of product distribution' and 'the greatest ever business opportunity'. These were big claims which somehow seemed to make complete sense to me. It was very exciting and I walked out of the meeting three feet in the air.

What amazes me, looking back on that evening and the years that followed, was that I did not ask for any facts substantiating these huge claims; after all I am a person who needs proof. Having come from a military engineering, banking and consulting background, you would think I would need solid evidence on these claims about Network Marketing's future. My friends and family thought I had either gone crazy or been duped into joining some pyramid scheme.

In reality, it wasn't until I ran a Network Marketing trade association in the early 1990s and had to discuss the industry with British government officials and journalists, did I realise how poor my understanding of this industry was. I was not alone. In fact, I was unable to find one person who could explain the Network Marketing industry in a credible manner. The industry lacked what is known as a 'strategic' vision.

Everyone needs a Strategic Vision

In such a young industry, the lack of Strategic Vision is not surprising, yet the problem is that people struggle to invest today if they have no clear confident vision of the future. It creates a short term attitude and lack of commitment, that assures failure in most people.

If you write a business plan for your bank or investors, the first section is always a Strategic Vision on the industry you are involved with. It provides the basis for your business and thus the excitement and confidence you have in that business or career.

Every large company in the world develops its own strategic vision of their industry – both product and distribution. Research companies produce industry reports outlining their strategic vision. Strategic consultancies redesign organisations based on their strategic vision of that industry. This strategic work is recognised as being so important that they are the highest paid consultants in the world.

Using the analytical skills learnt as a strategic consultant, I produced my own Strategic 'Big Picture' Vision of the Network Marketing industry in 1992. I presented my vision to hundreds of thousands of people including government officials, business people and financial journalists (who, incidentally, must be the most sceptical people on the planet). Not one person has ever questioned its accuracy, logic or deductions so I am very confident about its validity.

Global Boom

The global boom in Network Marketing I predicted occurred [fortunately] now involving 50 million people with sales over US$100billion in 100 countries of the world. It reflected my often quoted passage from Victor Hugo... *Nothing, not all the armies in the world, can stop an idea whose time has come.*

New strategic vision

In the early 2000s, I noticed new developments which reflected the end of this growth boom. Not just that industry growth had slowed, there were other major strategic changes occurring. The famous pioneer CEOs retired and, for the first time, there was industry-wide restructuring.

I was excited as I knew this was a fundamental change in Network Marketing and I needed to conduct a new strategic analysis of the industry to develop my new 'Big Picture' of the future. I was excited because the Growth Stage of the industry's Lifecycle had arrived. The biggest growth period in an industry's future.

As I will explain, there are four primary trends driving the industry onwards and this growth is likely to last for at least twenty years. This confirms that Network Marketing is the 'Right' industry. I will then simply explain how industry's develop based on a Lifecycle Graph using lots of industry examples to show you why the timing is perfect of Network Marketing today. This will confirm the <u>Right Place at the Right Time</u>.

Lastly, I am going to explain some key points to help you determine what is the <u>Right Business</u> to join as this matters very much in the Growth Stage. Only the strong companies succeed and weak companies perish.

Intrapreneurs Rule OK!

The central theme throughout this book is that the business of Network Marketing is starting to boom and will be driven by a wave of Intrapreneurs. These Intrapreneurs have always been interested in Network Marketing yet haven't driven the business because the industry has been dominated by Entrepreneurs and the systems weren't proven enough for them. Intrapreneurs are the bulk of the opportunity seekers and so they will provide the force behind the big growth in the business.

Network Marketing is a simple business that anyone can succeed in. Whether you want to improve your lifestyle or make a fortune, it is all possible.

Many people struggle to believe this statement yet I assure you it is true. In countless companies and countries, I have met successful people from every sex, age, religion, background, disability and educational level.

I trust this simple book will provide that basic understanding of this industry to give you the belief in its future. Network Marketing is currently growing in nearly every country in the world. A situation that has never happened before. Strong companies are booming again and the evidence is overwhelming that Network Marketing is now destined for dramatic growth.

I make no excuses about my enthusiasm, I am more excited about my involvement in this industry now than I have been for twenty years, since my friend first introduced me to the concept. And this book will tell you why.

I hope you enjoy it.

Ed

Dedicated to Vicky, of course

Published by 100% Success Institute Ltd.

First published in New Zealand by 100% Success Institute Ltd,
415 Remuera Road, Remuera Village, Auckland, New Zealand. www.ludbrook.com

Cartoons by Mick Davis
Designed and Typeset by Lee Kretschmar

ISBN 978-0-9582913-23

Contents

What is Network Marketing?

The new secret of success is distribution, distribution, distribution.
The Economist 28th Feb 1998

After years of being a quiet achiever, Direct Sales has been propelled into the spotlight by the brash new Internet based companies that are 'selling direct'; companies like Dell Computers and Amazon.com. Their influence has turned 'selling direct' into the hottest industry in the world and in doing so turned the 100 year old traditional Direct Sales industry on its head.

Direct Sales is a method of distributing consumer products and services directly to the customer. Instead of selling through shops, Direct Sales uses a marketing network of self-employed people to find customers and move products. They are known as Associates, Consultants, Distributors, Independent Business Owners, ISP, Members or Representatives.

Network Marketing is the dominant form of Direct Sales where there are two opportunities; the first is the Direct Sales income opportunity to build a customer base. The other is a business opportunity to develop a Marketing Network from which you will earn commissions on the sales of multiple levels of Networkers. This is why it used to be called Multi-Level Marketing, or MLM.

Your Network of Business Partners

The excitement of Network Marketing is that even with no joining restrictions and limited investment, there is the possibility to create an enormous and residual income. The flexibility of the opportunity allows for incomes from a few hundred dollars to millions from the same basic Network Leadership franchise concept.

The Magic Formula

Bill Gates, of Windows and Microsoft fame, is one of the richest men in the world and he made his fortune by his early forties. So how did he make so much money so quickly?

He wasn't in the computer software business when it started. He wasn't even born when it started.
He isn't that much brighter than you or me.
He doesn't work that much harder than you or me.
He didn't start with lots of money. He set up Microsoft in his garage.

He has been so successful because he was in the <u>right place</u> at the <u>right time</u>. He joined the computer software industry as it started to boom. Anita Roddick of Body Shop fame was the same. She joined the Natural Cosmetics and Franchising industries [right place] at the right time.

Behind every fortune in the world, is the first step of the Magic Formula for success – you must be in the **Right Place at the Right Time**. If you get this strategic factor correct, you are positioned to ride a boom in an industry.
A rapidly growing industry creates opportunities of everyone, not just the owners of the leading companies. Everyone involved has an opportunity to make extra-ordinary incomes and wealth.
Without rapid growth, above-average income opportunities disappear for the average person. Not only this, the excitement of a growth industry disappears, leaving you with the normal politics and stress of a normal tedious industry.

Lesson One for a Life of Excitement and Above-Average Income – You must join a HIGH Growth industry [Right Place] at the Right Time.

The Right Business

Many people have incredible success stories from pioneering a boom industry such as videos, the internet or mobile phones. Exciting stories of businesses doubling every 3 months and company parties that lasted for days. The owners show you pictures of Ferraris in the garage, helicopters on their lawn and exotic holidays. The employees smile at those crazy adrenalin-filled days.

The sad reality is that less than 1% of these companies survived. Less than 1% of the owners got rich and those crazy exciting work days have become a distant memory. Being in the Right Place at the Right Time is VITAL for success and you can experience a boom YET without the Right Business [system and management], you will still experience failure.

I know this seems obvious yet you would be amazed how many people get so excited about a concept and timing, they ignore analysing the Business. This does not mean going into details, yet everyone should be very clear on the opportunities the industry presents combined with how and why the Business will exploit those opportunities. For a good company, it is simple to analyse whether it will be able to exploit opportunities.

> ***Lesson Two – Analyse the Business you join.***
> ***Will it succeed in the pressure of High Growth industry?***

Massive Action

The last part of the Formula is taking Massive Action.

Ask ANY successful person how hard they worked in the early days of their career or business and you will hear many stories of personal sacrifice. All success requires a price to be paid in time and effort. The fact is that ONLY massive action creates the results necessary to succeed in a new opportunity. To think any differently, is crazy. Incidentally it's also great fun to be in a company that is riding a boom.

The Magic Success Formula
- **Right Place**
- **Right Time**
- **Right Business**
- **Massive Action**

Strategy 1.0

I would love to be the first person to reveal this 'Magic Formula' to the world yet it's actually the most basic principle of business strategy – Make sure your business is in the Right part of an industry at the Right time with the Right business model. This is Strategy 1.0!

The Right Business starts with the Right Strategy

Every large company in the world has a 'strategy team' evaluating their industry and business to determine if their strategy is correct. If they are happy with the analysis, it gives the business confidence to invest the resources needed. It gives the management confidence to drive the business forward.

Business Planning

Another way to look at this is for business planning. If you have ever written a Business Plan, the first part of the document should be your 'Strategic Vision' of the 'Current Situation' and then the expected 'Future Development' of your industry. From this analysis, you will then explain why the Business model you have will succeed.

No Bank or investor will ever give you money until they are confident of your strategy. Management, finances, marketing, etc are very important to your success YET nothing is more important than your strategy.

One Simple Lesson

Amazingly less than 1% of those who join the Network Marketing industry can explain why the industry will grow and the real opportunities it presents. They cannot tell you why they are confident about the future other than their excitement in their company.

They lack this 'Strategic Vision' so can never be confident about the future of the industry. By reading this book, you are conducting all the strategic analysis on Network Marketing you will ever need to do in one simple lesson.

No Commitment

Without a clearly understood vision of the industry's future, and how your business fits within this, how can anyone truly commit to invest the time, effort and money to build today for results in the future?

It is, therefore, not surprising that most people take a very short term outlook on their Network Marketing business. They commit for a few months [or a few weeks!] And quit before they ever had a chance of success. What makes me angry is that they then blame their company or the industry for their failure! In reality, they have been unprofessional.

For years, crowds of Networkers have agreed that it is normal in every career and business, for there to be a learning and building period. Normally, income will be low in this period. In fact, often there will be no income or investment. People are happy to do this because they have a confident vision of the medium and long term results for their investment in the short term.

Building Confidence

Network Marketing is a High Income opportunity with a long term future. However, you must do some Strategic Analysis. If you do not already know how to do this, then this book will teach you all you need to know.

The result will give you Confidence.

Confidence to invest your time and effort to build a network business without expecting quick results. Confidence to keep working as you experience disappointment while simultaneously learning the skills necessary to succeed. As the famous business author Rosabeth Kantor put it so beautifully, you need to believe your strategy ...

' inspire confidence in advance of victory, in order to attract the investments that make victory possible'

Strategy in action

Rubber Boots to European giant

When the Finns look at the incredible success of Nokia, they laugh that their old rubber boot company has been so successful. Nokia started its life making rubber boots by the 1980's it was already a leader in electronics.

Then it took a new visionary CEO Jorma Ollila to strategically position Nokia at the start of the 1990's to be at the heart of the mobile phone business. Ollila knew that mobile phone industry was the "Right Place at the Right Time". His brilliance was then manifested through his business concept. He got rid of other non-telecoms divisions and developed a unique product strategy where mobile phones were considered an exciting consumer product with great design and functionality. This was a departure from the strategy of the other mobile suppliers, such as Ericsson, championed their 'technology' over design and functionality. This was because these companies were originally telecom technology companies, rather than consumer electronics businesses.

The incredible mobile industry growth of the 1990's confirmed that both Nokia and Eriksson were in the Right Place at the Right Time. The difference between Nokia and other mobile phone companies was that consumers preferred their exciting phones to the technically more advanced phones, like Eriksson. The Right Strategy created the Right Business!

By the end of the 1990's, Nokia was the most valuable company in Europe and its employees were cashing in billions of euro's of shares. At the same time Ericsson were closing factories and retrenching thousands of employees.

Nokia was in the Right Industry at the Right Time with the Right Business

The lesson to be learnt from Nokia is that success is more than just being in the right industry, you must have the right business as well.

Right Place

Trendsurfing

'A fad is a wave in the ocean, and a trend is the tide. A fad gets a lot of hype, and a trend gets very little.

Like a wave a fad is very visible, but is goes up and down in a big hurry. Like the tide, a trend is almost invisible, but it's very powerful over the long term'

'The 22 Immutable Laws of Marketing', Reis and Trout

Being in the 'Right Place' is about long-term growth potential. Industries with the biggest futures are those positioned ahead of the strongest trends, which I call Primary Trends. Primary Trends are so fundamental and powerful that they are often referred to as Revolutions: The Information Revolution, The Learning Revolution, The Socialist Revolution.

For Network Marketing to be a major growth industry of the future it needs to be driven by Primary Trends. **Primary Trends are mainly found in four key economic areas. They are:**

1. **What makes people happy?**
2. **How do we make money?**
3. **How companies sell?**
4. **How people buy?**

I will explain what is happening in each area and what the Primary Trends are. In reality they will quickly reveal themselves. Obviously, four Primary Trends are behind Network Marketing or I wouldn't be writing this book. They will confirm the 'Right Place' element of the entrepreneur's magic formula.

A trend is a direction that a lot of consumers, the leading-edge consumers, are taking - the general drift of the marketplace. Trends are important if you want to position a product (or yourself) in the market and appeal to people in the language they are now or will be taking.

'The Popcorn Report', Faith Popcorn

Right Time

The Industry Lifecycle

Any student of economics, management or marketing will know that all industries grow in an Industry Lifecycle. By understanding the basics of an Industry Lifecycle you can estimate when is the Right Time to join.

An industry Lifecycle is traditionally split into five distinct Development Stages: Birth, Establishment, Growth [sometimes called Shakeout], Maturity and Decline. Each new stage requires a specific strategy to succeed which was different from the strategy used to develop the Stage that preceded it.

The Establishment and Growth stages are when an industry booms and the fortunes are made. They are similar environments yet companies and people do require different strategies to be successful.

1. <u>Birth Stage.</u> **Innovator-pioneer led.** This is when the pioneers create the central concept of an industry, like the early software pioneers developed programming languages rather than actual software programmes.
2. <u>Establishment Stage.</u> **Entrepreneur led.** A few companies 'takeoff'. Their success attracts numerous entrepreneurs who establish new markets in 'growth at all costs' strategy. Low profitability produces very low success rates.
3. <u>Growth Stage.</u> **Intrapreneur led.** The industry is established so the strategic focus changes to productivity and profitability. A 'dominant' business model drives evolution. Strong companies flourish, weak die. Revenues and profits rocket.
4. <u>Maturity Stage.</u> Industry dominated by a few competitors.
5. <u>Decline Stage.</u> Competition increases between remaining competitor companies.

Obviously the biggest rewards go to those who join in the two early Stages. The challenge is that you have a tiny chance of success and must accept highest risks to succeed. Most people want to avoid risk yet still have high rewards so they should join an industry at the start of the Growth Stage.

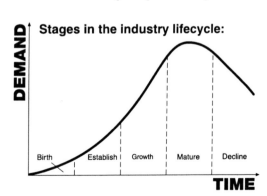

Stages in the industry lifecycle:

DEMAND / Birth / Establish / Growth / Mature / Decline / TIME

Growth Stage = High reward for Low risk

Primary Trend #1
What's important in life?

Lifestyle Revolution

The motivation behind all of our behaviour is the pursuit of happiness. Faith Popcorn, arguably the world's leading trend-spotter, conducts her primary research by asking this simple question ...

Are you happy?

She finds that this question opens the flood gates to what people really think and feel. To answer they reveal their inner-most concerns and desires that will drive their behaviour in the future.

Are you happy with your income?
Are you happy with your home?
Are you happy with your relationships?
Are you happy with your security?
Are you happy with yourself?

Ask yourself some 'Are you happy?' questions.

The fact is that most people are unhappy with their life. After spending so much time madly working to pay for that better house, better car and foreign holiday, few feel wealthier. Economists can prove we are financially wealthier but they cannot measure the poverty of the soul.

Feeling unfulfilled is a major trend. People are giving up excellent salaries in the cities to move to towns and places where they take less demanding jobs to 'spend time with the family' or 'for a better quality of life'. People are taking jobs where they get more 'personal satisfaction', or 'personal freedom' and are starting their own businesses because 'they always wanted to'. Above all we desire flexibility and substance in our life.

The personality cult of glamour and fame will slowly die as we realise how shallow that existence is. Character traits of honesty, integrity and trust are becoming important again as they offer the only solution to long term happiness and self-esteem. Looking good is no replacement for feeling good. People in general want a better life and they want a better lifestyle.

To reinforce this you will find, in the first pages of nearly every economic textbook what economists call the 'basic economic problem'.

> *'Human existence has been preoccupied with the production and consumption of wealth, the desire for which seems to arise from man's basic impulse to increase his lifestyle (my word). The concepts of wealth and lifestyle, therefore, stand at the heart of economics.'*
> **An Introduction to Modern Economics, Longman, 1992.**
> **Hardwick, Khan and Mead,**

Wealth is cars, houses, money, businesses and the other things you buy and own.

Lifestyle is the enjoyment you get from these things and how you live your life around them.

There is a limit to our time and effort. Depending on our aspirations, we focus on either Wealth or Lifestyle. We focus on what is important to us at the time.

After World War 2 we were poor and so we focused on creating wealth. Having a great lifestyle was not a priority. We advanced so rapidly that by the 1960's we decided to enjoy ourselves, hence the 'swinging sixties'. Life was so good that we were unprepared for the oil and business shocks of the 1970's. This resulted in new national leaders who promised wealth with stability. Leaders such as Thatcher, Kohl, Mitterrand, Reagan and Nakasone sang a song of expansion, economic efficiency and financial opportunity. They pointed the way to 'true capitalism' and society became fixated on wealth creation whatever the cost.

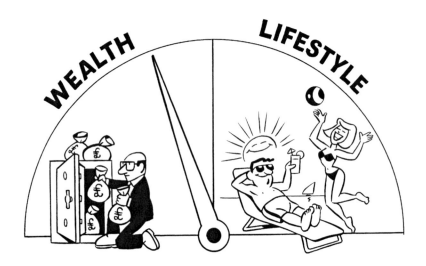

The eager 1990's

'He who dies with the most toys wins.' Car sticker

The 1980's saw the dawn of the new Information Age. Service sectors such as PR, banking, publishing, computing and advertising exploded into activity, especially in the 1990's. A return to economic strength was reflected in the booming stock and property markets. We bought houses, cars, shares and other assets. With new technology such as fibre optics and the silicon chip, this era made us richer, faster than ever before. Inefficient and uncompetitive industries faltered and business cycles which used to take 20 years took only 5 years as technology sped up the world. These were exciting times.

The bubble finally burst, bringing many people back to earth. Following the quagmire of recession and unemployment, many are analysing whether this 'rush for money' made them happy. We have started to look again for quality of life. Relationships and spirituality are being discussed openly again. The 21st century 'caring man' has been born and 'sixties' clothes and music are back in fashion. Welcome to the Lifestyle Revolution.

The Lifestyle Revolution

If you doubt the coming of the Lifestyle Revolution, you only have to look as far as the High Street. The 1960's are back. Platform shoes, miniskirts, psychedelic rock, 'granny glasses', flares and love beads are in fashion. The Beatles are back in the music charts and they have even run the Woodstock Music concert again!

New technology and communications will make the swing towards Lifestyle faster and stronger and create more momentum than any previous swing in history. Lifestyle is the new focus, so creating better Lifestyle is a major trend in society. It is so powerful that it has become a Primary Trend.

Network Marketing is in the forefront of the Lifestyle Revolution. You work when you like, where you like, as much as you like. It is completely flexible and works around you. It is also based on you making other people successful, whilst encouraging you to work on your own personal development. The Lifestyle Revolution is driving Network Marketing and anyone involved with it forward.

Network Marketing is in front of the Lifestyle Revolution. You work when you like, where you like, as much as you like.

Primary Trend #2
How do we make money?

The Self-employment Revolution

The Income Paradigm.

When it comes to making money, most people have what is called a *Job Paradigm*. A paradigm is the way you view a certain situation. The *Job Paradigm* is that you think that making money is based on having a 'good job'. This is now a dangerous view of making money because the world of work has changed forever and many jobs are under threat.

Today, you need an *Income Paradigm*. Instead of your focus being on a job, you need to look for opportunities to make an income. It is time to drop the blind allegiance to the sacred Job. The 'Job' has changed and it does not mean what it used to. Unfortunately for most of us, to reject the job paradigm is difficult because in the past it was the answer to long term happiness.

 The 'Job' has changed and it does not mean what it used to.

Are you a Dumb Frog ?

They say, if you drop a frog into a pot of hot water, it'll hop right out (smart frog).

Yet, if you put the frog into a pot of cold water first, then by applying heat, bring the water to the boil, the frog will happily stay there until it dies. (dumb frog)

Many people are currently thinking and acting like that dumb frog. The problem lies with the 'job paradigm' which assumes that a job is a source of income with long term security and many other benefits. Now that things have changed, the gas has been turned up under 'their pot'.

We spend years at schools, colleges and, for a few, University, to gain skills for life, more importantly, to get a 'good job'. People are ranked by their job. Parents push their children to 'get a job'. When political parties talk about improving people's lives, they talk about jobs.

> **FACT – Most people hate their job. They only go to work to earn money and the social aspects of their job.**

The reason is that in the past a job proved itself to be a *stable source of income* which gave you a better life. The better the job, the better the income, the better the life. You could rely on it, you had *long term security*. Some industries like steel, mining, ship building and government service took it further and a job became a 'Job for Life'. It also provided opportunities for promotion and other non-financial benefits, such as a sense of community, identity, challenge, achievement and growth

Our Job Paradigm became...

> Job = Income *plus*
> a Promise of Security *plus*
> a Promise of further Opportunities *plus*
> Other Benefits

For these additional promises and benefits, we put up with domineering bosses, unpaid overtime, discrimination , being told what to wear, when to work, when to turn up and when to go on holiday, etc., etc. We delegated the responsibility for much of our lives to our employer on the understanding that they would look after us.

The World is Flat

The title of Thomas Friedman's 2007 global business best-seller is *The World is Flat*. In the book, the three-times Pulitzer winning journalist simply explains that the predicted convergence of communications and computer technologies has finally occurred and we now compete globally.

We have already seen the impact of the new economies, such as China, on the manufacturing sector. 'Convergence' means that they can now compete in the high value service sector. Basically any job not requiring a physical presence can be out-sourced or off-shored to a low cost country. Everything from evaluating X-rays to mathematics coaching to aircraft design.

Technology and global markets have improved our lives in many ways. They have also destroyed the unwritten 'job promise' forever. Many of us feel 'let down' by organisations and the government because they have broken their job promises. The reality is that they were promises they would never be able to keep anyway.

In today's markets, companies have to be more efficient in everything, especially the labour-force. Labour is now a global market so employees in Manchester have to compete with those in Malaysia. Productivity is the watchword - it refers to 'How much an employee produces and at what cost'. If employees cannot be competitively productive then their company will make that person/team/division/factory redundant and find a more efficient solution.

If unions think they are going to fight that economic reality, then they are dreaming. We can see them trying in Germany and Australia but they are only delaying the inevitable. Employers have little choice; they are competitive or they die. The economic disasters of Eastern Europe are a classic example of what happens if you try to fight the global market.

> *Many of us feel 'let down' by organisations and the government because they have broken their promises. The reality is that they were promises they would never be able to keep anyway.*

Professor Handy, the internationally renowned business guru, calls this time 'The Age of Unreason' and suggests that the way we make our money in the future will be very different from the past. In short, a new paradigm. If you want security, development opportunities, challenge, achievement and increasing benefits do not look to the job world.

In the new economic world, companies are having to:
1. **Pay more for high tech, high value employees.**
2. **Pay everyone else less.**
3. **Replace people, especially management, administration and manual labour workers with new technology.**
4. **Employ part-time or contract workers who do not have the same social commitments as far as redundancy, training, pension, sick pay and holidays.**

Who are the winners?

The winners in the new 'flat world' are capitalists. The people who own the assets. The people that own or control the companies that can exploit the new global markets and new efficiencies. It's obvious that the Rich are Getting Richer. The economic losers are nearly everyone else.

This is a general statement yet the challenge for the 'employed' sector is clear. Let's look at the implications:

Core Worker Pressure

Core Workers are those employees who could be considered assets or value of a company. They are the people who hold the valuable 'people element' of a company like important client relationships, specific skills or abilities.

These valuable employees will continue to be better paid and receive more benefits as long as their value cannot be 'out-sourced' to a lower cost base. As they become more valuable, they receive more responsibilities and more stress. And it's the stress that is seriously affecting the health and lifestyle of many Core Workers.

When you relate this to the Lifestyle trend, you can see why so many core workers and professionals are looking for ways to get out of the 'Rat Race' and to have a better Lifestyle.

'If you win the Rat Race, you are still a Rat'

Lily Tomlin

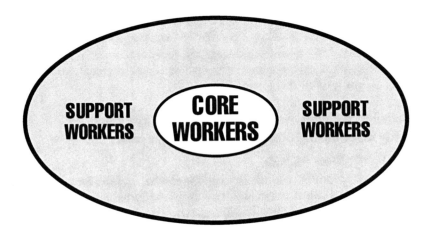

Support Workers

Support Workers are not vital to the company. They make up the bulk of most companies as they fill the ranks of management, administration, finance, manufacturing, service and other systemised areas. They are the real victims of this change in business. It is their wages and positions which are being slashed. There is no economic reason why things will get better.

The Middle Class

The middle classes all over the world have benefited from a boom in employment, economic activity and asset prices, such as house values. Personal debt has soared. Wages have exceeded productivity and house values have exceeded ability to pay and still have a lifestyle. Convergence means that any inefficiency will be discovered and punished more quickly than ever before.

Government Workers

Government Workers have the most to fear from a 'flat' world. After years of high tax revenues based on booming business through globalization, convergence will mean massive pressure to cut taxes as the middle classes and support workers need money. Government workers will be squeezed to provide this extra cash. They will be squeezed to create more services with less money.

Points to accept:

1. <u>Not changing is very expensive.</u> When companies and governments bury their heads in the sand and refuse to change they just delay the inevitable, making any changes more dramatic and painful for everyone else.

2. <u>No large industry is safe.</u> Even the safe, secure banking industry has made thousands redundant. There are no 'jobs for life'.

3. <u>Huge Under-Employment.</u> Unemployment figures are a scam as they do not include the millions of people, of all ages, on training schemes, unregistered for benefit, on part-time work or on low pensions. These people are the under-employed and are often the real casualties of the changing work place.

4. <u>Over 40s Are Over The Hill.</u> The Institute of Employment Consultants report that 75% of employers want candidates between 21-30 and 60% of them specify age limits. The over 50's are the least desired. Employers see them as over-qualified and over-priced.

5. <u>Living Longer.</u> What makes these realities uglier is that most people will live longer now, with the chances being that you will live until you are 70, 80 or 90 years old. People might find themselves in a position of having to survive for 10 to 30 years without strong cashflow and valued employment. The humiliation of poverty will visit over increasing numbers.

The Real Timebomb

The real timebomb in most developed countries are the expected costs of paying for the pensions and health-care of the Baby Boomers Generations.

Born between 1945 and 1965, the 'Baby Boomers' are starting to retire and are projected to require a huge proportion of government spending and many will be very poor for many decades. Many people live their lives struggling to survive on their incomes only to retire on approx 25% of that income! Poverty is so difficult when you are older.

This is a national crisis so large that most politicians refuse to confront it.

A New Paradigm

Forget the job paradigm. The only viable view on making money is an **INCOME paradigm.** Your focus should be 'how am I going to earn an income?' not 'where am I going to get a job?'. This new view on life should allow you to assess the potential of any job, business or educational opportunity in a realistic light.

Millions of people will need a new income for many reasons and many are being left in the cold by the Job or Employment market. They are therefore, forced to investigate **Self-Employment** in order to secure an income. The **movement toward self-employment is the next PRIMARY trend** which focuses on 'How We Make Money'.

> ## *Movement toward Self-employment is the next Primary Trend*

There are two types of people flooding into self-employment:

1. <u>**Want to.**</u> These are Core Workers fleeing the dog-eat-dog world. Remember Trend 1? They are looking for lifestyle and a more rewarding work environment.
2. <u>**Have to.**</u> These are the Support Workers [and a few collapsed Core Workers] who have to find self-employed opportunities.

Self-employed Opportunity Seekers

Most people do not understand the world of 'self-employment' or 'business opportunities.' For this reason, many make mistakes that waste a lot of their time, money and emotional strength. There are three sorts of people seeking a self-employed opportunity; **Part Time "Job" Seekers, Dream-chasers and Business Opportunity Seekers**

1. Part-timer "Job Seekers"

There are lots of people are looking to earn a little bit of extra money to improve their lifestyle for which they will invest a few hours a week to make a few hundred dollars. To understand the importance of this in people's lives read the section at the back of this book called 'The Real Power'.

They are not looking for a 'business opportunity'. No amount of promotion will convince them either. They are essentially looking for a **self-employed job opportunity.**

Some people take part-time jobs yet the work is rarely enjoyable or flexible enough. Tens of millions of people join a Direct Sales company [ie Network Marketing] as they can earn great cash WITH time flexibility and a very enjoyable environment. We are increasingly finding that the fun, personal development and friendship benefits of this opportunity is attracting people. Consequently the power of the Direct Sales opportunity provides the solid foundation upon which a Network Marketing business opportunity sits.

2. Dream-chasers

Dream chasers have a compelling vision for their lives and know what they want to do. Their passion or idea could be anything from opening a flower shop to creating new technology that will change the world. We need to applaud these people because they are taking action and chasing their dream. They are the entrepreneurs whose efforts often change our world for the better and in doing so inspire us to a better future.

3. Business Opportunity Seekers

The other large group of people are looking for more than the part-time opportunity of a bit of money. They are looking for a business or income stream that will change their lifestyle, inspire their lives or be a financial saviour. They are open to suggestions.

The Entrepreneurial Reality

Whether you are a dream-chaser or business opportunity seeker, there is an entrepreneurial reality that most would like to ignore. It is that being an entrepreneur and starting your own business is a very risky decision.

The US Commerce Commission reports that 80% of new businesses fail in the first 5 years with 40% failing in the first year. The fact is that most people do not have the money, knowledge, skills or confidence to succeed in their own business.

Taking Risks

Entrepreneurs are the life-force of business today. They are the risk-takers who exploit opportunities to start and grow businesses pioneering new products, markets and business strategies. They are the highest paid people in business yet they accept the biggest risks. They are the pioneers of our economy and the most admired business people. They are admired not just for the money they make and jobs they create, they are mainly admired because they are prepared to take risks most people are not.

Nearly everyone has at one time had a new product idea, business idea or seen an opportunity in the market. Unfortunately few will ever act on that opportunity because they are not prepared to take the risks inherent in starting a new business. Whilst many dream of rewards of being an entrepreneur, few are prepared to take the risks necessary to succeed as an entrepreneur. This is why most people should be **Intrapreneurs**.

Definition: Intrapreneurship

'is the practice of entrepreneurial skills and approaches within a company or at home.'

Wikipedia

An Intrapreneur exploits opportunities yet within the security of an established organisation, thus the term 'intra-entrepreneur'. Whilst potential rewards are lower than starting your own new venture, the risks are significantly reduced so the possibility of success is dramatically increased. It is a compromise that most people want to make.

Within a company, the 'Employee Intrapreneur' is a person who uses his entrepreneurial skills to exploit new opportunities for the organisation. They are not common.

The largest quantity of Intrapreneurs work for themselves yet in cooperatives, networks and the franchise industry. They gain the freedom of owning their own business yet also wants the security of a proven business working within a large corporate support organisation. They make up the vast majority of business opportunity seekers.

The Intrapreneur Machine

Intrapreneurs make up the bulk of the Business Opportunity Seekers. When an industry can appeal to them, they are an economic machine that will drive that industry forward. The obvious example has been the franchise industry who offers the blend of Opportunity With Security.

A franchisee is an Intrapreneur

They want to own their own business [franchise is old French for Freedom] yet, due to the risk, decide to buy a proven business system. They make this decision even though it means their expansion opportunities are restricted, they must pay fees and lose control of their business. They want someone else to take the pioneering risk and want to reduce risk through working within the franchise organisation.

The key marketing benefit of franchising is not 'get rich', it is a 'proven money making opportunity'. This is the most empowering benefit for an Intrapreneur and franchising has perfected it. Not surprising the Intrapreneurs have flooded into this industry for a couple of decades fuelling its global boom.

The 'People's Franchise'

People need some other form of income opportunity. They need a business where they don't have to have prior knowledge or skills to do it. A business where there is little capital investment involved and very low risk. A business where they are helped and supported as they learn and develop their livelihood. A business that does not discriminate for age, physical health, location, sex, experience, skills nor education.

People need a proven business system where they work on their own YET with others. Basically, what we are describing here is some sort of low cost franchise. A franchise that anyone can do, where everyone has a good chance of making money related to the time and effort they expend. A 'People's Franchise'.

Network Marketing is the only industry that offers a 'People's Franchise'. It is a new key industry and sits well in front of the PRIMARY trend towards self-employment. Self-employment is accelerating around the world as large groups of people continue to be excluded from the 'job' market. To them Network Marketing is a very attractive option.

Network Marketing is the only industry that offers a 'People's Franchise'

Primary Trend #3
How companies sell

Direct Shopping Revolution

The next area to investigate is the economy – how we make and sell products. Our newspapers are full of articles explaining the revolution in manufacturing which was first started in Japan and is now led by China. High technology, low wage costs and huge factories have reduced the cost of making products dramatically.

Whilst the changes in manufacturing are amazing, the Primary Trend is in how companies sell, or distribute, products. The big distributors now control the economy with their massive supermarkets, chain stores and product warehouses. They have had their revolution and the big new Trend is the consumer buying direct. This is the age of Direct Shopping and it is absolutely fundamental to the growth of Network Marketing.

For the average person, consumer goods and services are the businesses to be involved in whether you are making the product or distributing it. Manufacturing used to be the growth side of the business, now it is distribution. Professor Paul Pilzer in his book *'Should you quit before you are fired?'* explains why:

In the 1960's, the manufacturing proportion of a product's final price was typically about 50%, with distribution the other 50%. If the product cost $300, the manufacturing cost would be $150.

If the manufacturer made a 20% saving ($30) through new technology then he could reduce the price by $30 or keep the $30 as additional profits. These were attractive savings and this promoted the increased use of new technology.

Today, that $300 product's price has probably dropped to about $100 and, **more importantly, the manufactured proportion of the final price would be no more than 20%, more likely 10%. If the manufacturer applied new methods now and made a 20% saving, they'd reduce the price by only $4. On the other hand, a 20% saving applied to distribution would reduce the price by $16. Four times the profit for the same percentage improvement. The opportunities for creating wealth are in Distribution!**

	1960's		2000's	
Selling Price	$300	20% saving	$100	20% saving
Manufacturing	50%	$30	20%	$4
Distribution	50%	$30	80%	$16

Understanding Direct Shopping

'distribution will be the next consumer oriented revolution.
Direct shopping from the producer to you - bypassing the retailer
altogether, no middlemen, no stops along the way.'
The Popcorn Report

Manufacturers have two ways of distributing products:

- Retailing (customer to the shop) *or*
- Direct Shopping (shop to the customer)

Retailing

Most consumer products are distributed through retail outlets. The challenges for the retailing sector are endless with increased competition, rapid market changes and a disinterested, financially concerned public.

There has been a revolution in retailing where friendly, helpful high street and corner shops have been replaced by retail chains slugging it out with 'out of town' shopping malls, retail parks, warehouses and discount clubs. These are signs of a mature industry controlled by giant companies who spend millions enticing customers into their shops. Big retail organisations now control the access to the customers and hold the manufacturers to ransom.

Who controls Retailers?

The retail sector is now controlled by those who control the capital. Private equity funds, venture capitalists, stock markets and the rich buy and sell retail chains because their capital is the most powerful force. To satisfy the capitalists 'return on capital', big retail chains must grow in size and profits. So with the retail market barely growing, the giants must take sales from their competitors and cut costs. The main victims are the small retail shops, which are dying in their thousands.

Staff are being laid off in their tens of thousands. Those left over are barely paid enough to motivate them to serve and educate the customer. As competition increases, prices decline and so does quality. It is a spiral that will be the undoing of many retailers as the customer is not truly winning in this process. Customers will go elsewhere if offered an alternative.

Direct Shopping

Direct Shopping is the distribution alternative to retailing and it can be split into two forms;

1. Direct Marketing, and
2. Direct Selling.

Direct Marketing

The Internet and computer systems have allowed Direct Marketing companies to by-pass the retailer effectively and efficiently and this industry has boomed. The convenience of shopping by Internet, mail or phone has mass appeal with the Internet allowing this sector to expand rapidly into all aspects of business.

The Achilles Heel of Direct Marketing is its lack of human contact (face to face product explanation and demonstration) and the spiralling costs of building customer bases. It is becoming an extremely competitive market which means that the consumer is becoming increasingly bombarded with advertising and customer prospecting; this, in turn, reduces effectiveness and increases costs.

Whoever can solve these two problems will have significant success in the Digital Direct Shopping world of the future.

Direct Selling

Direct Selling has changed significantly in the last 20 years as new technology and techniques have vastly increased its potential for growth. Behind the scenes, the ugly sister of distribution has been having a dramatic makeover. Gone are the 'foot-in-the-door' salesmen. The Cinderella of the Direct Shopping Revolution has joined the party. Direct Selling is split into two categories;

1. **Single-level Marketing**

2. **Multi-level Marketing (MLM)**

'Single level or SLM' means that the direct sales people are only paid on their own personal sales. 'Multi-level or MLM' means that the direct salespeople, called 'Distributors' or 'Consultants', are paid on their own sales AND royalties on the sales of multiple levels of recruits in their network.

'Single level' is 'classic' Direct Sales. They are the masters of commission-only sales by perfecting the systems necessary to find, recruit, train and motivate a commission-only sales person going into a home.

Multi-level [or Network Marketing] evolved from Single Level and Network Marketing companies which still offer a sales or customer based income opportunity to all those that join. For most people who join, this customer opportunity is the primary source of income.

The MLM Evolution - Leadership

The essential difference between the two systems is how a company seeks to grow. Single level direct sales companies control the recruitment, training and support of their sales force. To manage the sales system, a Single-level company usually appoints an 'Area Manager' who develops that area.

Network Marketing companies subcontract these roles to their networkers, making them responsible for growth. They are not restricted to a set area. It is this **'Network Leader'** opportunity to grow the number of people in the business that offers the big money and creates the dynamism in Network Marketing.

For years, the 'single level' companies questioned 'Network companies' for the uncontrolled nature of their growth strategy. What they cannot question is the results. Network Marketing has grown many times faster than single level and now dominates the industry of Direct Sales.

In the USA, 97% of Direct Sales companies, people and revenues are from companies that use Network Marketing.
Direct Sales = Network Marketing

The key growth factor is the **Network Leader.** With the excitement of the Network Leadership opportunity and unlimited expansion, Network Leaders make a lot more money than Area Managers. Thus eventually many of the good Area Managers left the single level companies and became Network Leaders. It is not surprising that the grandlady of single level direct sales, Avon Inc, has now introduced a Network Leadership programme to replace its traditional Area Manager system.

The Power of Network Marketing is the Network Leaders

The rise of Direct Sales

For nearly fifty years, the essential business model of Direct Sales has barely changed. Innovations like the multi-level payment plan, direct representative ordering and computer efficiencies have had major impacts yet the fundamental model of *'representative selling and servicing customers'* has never changed.

Due to technological changes initiated by the Internet, the fundamental Direct Sales business model is changing. For the first time, we are seeing the large Direct Selling companies making root and branch changes to their global business models. We are seeing the emergence of a new era in Direct Sales.

Beating the Internet

It is easy to think that the Internet will dominate all other forms of distribution. Finding products and buying is so simple. Home distribution systems are getting better every year. Yet for all of the claims made by the Internet gurus, it has not destroyed the retail sector, nor will it destroy Network Marketing.

In the competitive business of distributing products, the most critical part of the process is finding, educating and inspiring customers. Here Network Marketing is king. No shop, website or catalogue will ever come close to an individual enthusiastically presenting a product directly to another person. Especially, if that promoter 'personally recommends the product through own use.'

Final Evolutionary Step...

All distribution systems develop an all-powerful business model where everyone involved is fairly rewarded. This is when a business model achieves its true power and growth explodes.

All systems together

The ultimate Direct Shopping opportunity takes the best of all forms of Direct Shopping:

1. From Single-level Marketing, it has a great part-time or full-time income opportunity. This will be either a sales or catalogue order opportunity. This creates the customer volume.
2. From Multi-level Marketing, it has a great Network Leader business opportunity. This creates the growth.
3. From Direct Marketing, it has a great customer support programme to create ongoing customer sales and loyalty. This also creates income security.

Primary Trend #4
How consumers buy

The Consumer Experience Revolution

You are exposed to 250 advertisements every day!

Everywhere you look there are advertisements; newspapers, radio, internet, buses, buildings, lifts, school books, beer glasses, rubbish bins. We are being advertised to death. Information overload.

For every need, desire or want there is a product. Not just one product but a multitude of options, varieties and choices. Go into a local shop for black socks and you will find not just one type, they will be high cut, low cut, woollen, cotton, etc, etc. endless options. Type 'black socks' into Google and you get 17,900,000 responses in 0.27seconds. How do you decide?

Endless advertisements, products, prices, special offers. Lots of choices does not make decision making easier. It creates the greatest problem for consumers today – CONFUSION.

In the confusion of our over-marketed world, we are losing that shopping experience. We are losing our ability to process the flood of information so lose our power to choose. We are losing the inspiration in shopping. Like so many other things in our modern life; shopping is becoming stressful.

What do confused consumers do? They lose their power to choose the right product for them at the right price. They buy products on recognition and trust, commonly known as Brands. This means they often buy the wrong product [normally at a higher price]. Or do not buy at all!

Primary Trend....

The Primary Trend in Consumer behaviour is a desire for a 'trusted' shopping experience - The Consumer Experience Revolution. They want clear information. They want 'trusted' recommendations. They want inspiring products, packaging and a shopping experience.

Network Marketing is the best marketing channel to deliver this consumer desire. It delivers a unique shopping experience directly to the consumer's home. Highly motivated people want to create a positive experience. They produce the information customers need and have the time to explain the products. They also have personal examples of product value to inspire consumers to purchase.

Everyone wins!

Network Marketing is a relatively small method of distribution when compared to Retailing, but it offers huge expansion possibilities, as it is now attractive to consumers, manufacturers and participants alike.

Customers win

The customer benefits enormously. Firstly, the convenience of the shop coming to the home. Secondly, professional education on the products. Finally, a personal after sales service. The customer also buys from someone who actually uses the product so the immense power of 'word-of-mouth' advertising comes into play. No other form of distribution even comes close in these areas and companies are continually improving their service standards and guarantees.

Manufacturers win

Network Marketing is a manufacturer's dream because their product is taken directly to the customer's home. The customer is educated on their product alone. The manufacturer also gets customer and product sales information much faster as they become much 'closer' to the customer. They have gained back some control. As sales staff are remunerated on a "commission only" sales basis, they are much more motivated to succeed.

Participants win

New technology, products and remuneration systems means the business has changed, thus increasing the rewards and the chances of success.

Network Marketing offers the best win-win situation for all elements in the economic chain. Other forms of distribution are not fulfilling the changing needs of the customer and, inevitably, those guys decide the rules of the distribution game. The timing has not been right for Network Marketing to come into the limelight until now. It's only now that we have busier lives, job insecurity, a competitive global market and new technology that makes this kind of distribution able to compete with retailing.

It's a win-win situation for everyone!

'the highest paid person in the first half of this century will be the story-teller.'

Rolf Jensen, Danish Futurist

Rolf Jensen was not describing author's such as Harry Potter's JK Rowling. He was describing the rise of the business story-teller, the most powerful people in consumer marketing.

The 20th century was the 'consumer century'. The masses went from spending on purely basics at the start of the century to their great-grand children being able to afford products once only available to the rich. The market responded by creating every consumer product the mind could imagine, in every variation possible.

By the 21st century the consumer has endless choices so competition in the consumer market is based on who can excite the consumer either through commodity selling [big shops with simple products at lowest prices] or through story-telling [explaining the value of your product in an inspiring way.]

The Power of Story Telling...

An old European folk story tells of an old man who had fallen on hard times and his possessions were being sold by auction to pay his debts. The next possession for sale was the man's beloved violin.

The auctioneer asked for bids and the room was silent. Lower and lower went the price he offered the violin with no interest shown until he was nearly giving the violin away.

The old man was distraught as he imagined his prized violin was being given away for nothing. The old man stood and shouts 'Stop! Stop! Give me the violin.'

So he stands on the auction stand, brings the violin to his chin and starts playing the most beautiful music. The crowd were entranced by the music and, seizing the moment, the auctioneer shouted 'who will start the bidding for this lovely instrument!'

As the old man played the music, the bidding exploded into action as the people were inspired by the opportunity of creating such wonderful music. The violin was sold for a lot of money.

Like the old man and his violin, people need to be inspired to 'buy' these days. The choices are endless. The opportunities for creating new wealth for average people are based on new products and new ways to sell them. The key to success is communication. Positive communication. No pressure, just inspiration, in fact, story-telling.

No business is more designed to harness the power of inspiring communication than Network Marketing. Here you will find the highest paid story-tellers of the 21st century.

Professor Miller's famous Paper

In 1956, in what is often referred to as the 'greatest ever paper written in the history of psychology', Professor George Miller published a paper on how our brains deal with choice and when they get confused and make mistakes.

By studying psychological experiments of sight, taste, smell, hearing, etc, he noticed that we can only hold a certain number of options in our short term memory. If there are more options then we get confused and make mistakes. He called his paper - 'The Magical Number Seven, Plus Minus Two.'
Seven was the number of options that we can hold in our short term memory. Seven was the clarity before confusion.

So what do people need today to help them gain the Power to Choose properly – the answer is Seven! It is the number of clarity, simplicity and order. There has always been something Magical in Seven as Professor Miller concluded in his famous article,

'And finally, what about the magical number seven? What about the seven wonders of the world, the seven seas, the seven deadly sins, the seven daughters of Atlas in the Pleiades, the seven ages of man, the seven levels of hell, the seven notes to a musical scale and the seven days of the week?

What about the seven-point rating scale, the seven categories for absolute judgement, the seven objects in the span of attention and the seven digits in the span of immediate memory? For the present I propose to withhold judgement. Perhaps there is something deep and profound behind all these sevens, something just calling out for us to discover it.'

Lesson – When you deal with people, never offer more than seven options or you risk creating confusion.

The Right Place!

There are four Primary Trends in society today and only one industry, Network Marketing, sits in front of all four 'revolutions':

- **The Lifestyle Revolution**
- **The Self-employment Revolution**
- **The Direct Shopping Revolution**
- **The Consumer Experience Revolution**

These powerful trends will drive big growth in Network Marketing in the coming years. It is the only growth business which offers the average person opportunity, security and many other non-financial benefits. It truly is 'The People's Franchise'.

It is not some revolutionary form of business. It is a method of distributing consumer products which has developed over time so that it is 'the right place' to be for people looking for an income.

Network Marketing's friend - Technology

- Network Marketing's greatest friend is technology and the change that it creates.
- Technology has created so much wealth that we are now focusing on Lifestyle to make us happy.
- Technology has destroyed the established paradigm of job security and opportunities.
- Technology has thrown up distribution as the business to be revolutionised next.
- Technology has allowed Network Marketing to grow through its compensation plan.
- In today's changing world, I would prefer to have technology and change as my partners, rather than my enemies.

'it's clear that the concept of lifecycle stages has a significant impact on business strategy and performance'

Management Encyclopaedia

Right Time – Boom Time

The *Trend Journal* said it all...

'Timing is everything'

You can have the most powerful trends in the world driving your industry but if you join at the wrong time in the wrong way, you are likely to fail. Get it right and the momentum of the market place will create growth opportunities where even an ordinary person can create extraordinary results.

As we explained in the first Chapter, all industries develop in distinct developmental stages through what is called an Industry Lifecycle. Understanding the basics of an **Industry Lifecycle** is very important in determining the time to join an industry and the best strategy to use.

The basic rule is 'the earlier you join an industry, the bigger the opportunity yet the bigger the risk'.

Join an industry early and you had better be one of those bull headed, rhino-skinned pioneers who get a kick out of creating new opportunities. They are the bruisers, the self-starters, the visionaries who are prepared to take the knocks, the failures and the rejection.

Join an industry late and the opportunities for the average person to earn growth-driven extra-ordinary profits have gone.

For the average person [what we call the Intrapreneur], the best time to join is at the start of the Growth Stage. Whilst you could make more money joining in the Birth and Establishment stages, the chances of success are very small.

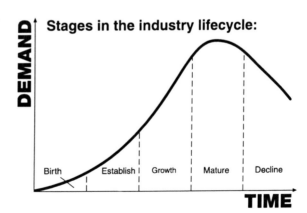

Stages in the industry lifecycle:

DEMAND

Birth | Establish | Growth | Mature | Decline

TIME

The Growth Stage in other industries

Personal Computers [PC]

The personal computer or PC was born in the late 1970's. Invented by IBM, the PC boom was then led by Apple with their unique Apple 2 then Macintosh PCs. Other companies, like Wang and Commodore, joined the boom as organisations discovered the joys of computing. The PC industry grew rapidly around the world using different operating systems, microprocessors and software platforms.

Those using PCs will remember that the product was flawed as computers often 'crashed' leaving users frustrated and annoyed. Customer service was non-existent!

In the mid 1980's, Intel and Microsoft finally created a 'dominant' operating system called 'Wintel' and thus they could grow the industry in a new way. They sold the PC as a consumer product instead of 'technology for organisations'.

With the Wintel system inside their PCs, the public began to trust the PC and embrace computing. Led by some old companies and new companies like Compaq, Acer and Dell, the PC industry exploded into growth. Within 10 years, a PC was placed on every desk and in many homes.

Lesson – Confidence in the PC product created the growth boom in the 1990's.

The period from 1970's to late 1980's was the 'Establishment Stage' of the PC industry. From late 1980's to late 1990's, was the Growth Stage. The core strategy needed for success was based on selling consumer PCs using the Wintel system. Apple ignored this and paid the price. Other companies tried to create new systems to compete with Wintel and all of them failed.

The PC industry has now entered its Maturity Stage. Price is the new strategy key to success. Dell Computers' direct selling model created the lowest prices so it became the largest PC company in the world. The Chinese are the lowest cost manufacturers thus a Chinese company has bought IBM's PC division. Now even Dell's direct model is being questioned as PCs enter a new Internet Age.

Mobile Phones

In the **Birth Stage** of Mobile phones, the telephones were heavy, expensive, unreliable and focused on business users. They were so heavy, most people had them in their cars so were known as a 'carphone'. Thus the UK's largest mobile retailer is known as the Carphone Warehouse.

Nokia understood that the biggest opportunity was selling mobile phones to consumers and led the mobile phone boom in the early to mid 1990s. What we would call the **Establishment Stage**. This was a period of dramatic numbers of mobile shop openings and countless special offers to get people to start using a mobile phone.

By the late 1990's it was clear that Nokia's strategy of selling simple attractive phones was the winning formula versus phones that had the best technology. This strategy became accepted by all suppliers and it was not surprising to see Ericssons 'technology led' mobile division merge with the world's leading consumer electronics' brand, creating Sony-Ericsson. The market entered its next **Growth Stage** and the mobile market boomed from the late 1990s into the 2000's.

Lesson – Confidence in the consumer product led to the growth boom in the late 1990's and early 2000's.

Internet

The concept of the Internet started in the 1970's and it wasn't until the mid 1990's that it entered its Establishment Stage, commonly known at the 'Dot Com Boom'. Hundreds of billions of dollars were poured into new ideas with little focus on profits.

Not surprisingly, the party eventually finished with billions lost as companies collapsed. Yet the Internet has not collapsed and millions have confidence in email, online buying and searching for information. The companies based on normal business principles have continued to grow and produce new profits. In the areas where the Internet has an advantage, sales are exploding.

Lesson – Confidence in using the Internet for email, online buying and searching led to the growth boom in the 2000's.

Franchising

The best industry that demonstrates how the Growth stage will develop in Network Marketing is it's closest business relation, Franchising. It also offers a self-employed opportunity for Intrapreneurs based on a proven system [a franchise].

How Franchising developed

The Birth Stage of Franchising started in the 1850's and the concept was actively pioneered following WW2 as entrepreneurs searched for ways to expand their businesses across the USA in the 1950's.

The Establishment Stage began in the 1960's, as people like Ray Kroc of McDonalds Corp had proven his franchised restaurant concept and was selling it across the USA. The news had spread and new franchise systems selling every different type of product you could imagine were being offered by entrepreneurs everywhere. The franchise industry boomed.

Entrepreneurial Weakness

All industries need entrepreneurs to establish and drive growth. The challenge was that by the end of the 1960's, many franchisors had begun focusing more on the sale of franchises than on supporting and operating successful franchise systems. Others made misrepresentations in how they recruited prospective franchisees. The result was an excessively high failure rate in franchisees.

Given the significant investment to buy a franchise, this failure rate resulted in a very negative public image and governmental action against the industry. It is claimed that even the US Congress came within a few votes of banning franchising!

One should also remember that a high failure rate is understood and accepted by entrepreneurs. They have a different mentality to the vast majority of the population; a mentality which makes them courageous entrepreneurs!

Pyramid Selling

One of the most famous 'innovations' in franchising and business opportunities at the time was the development of multi-level opportunities, known as 'pyramid selling'. These were purely recruiting schemes with near 100% failure rates and were rightly attacked by the media and governments.

Franchising Evolves

Governments are historically poor at regulating entrepreneurial activity yet they did their best to force franchise companies to provide more information about the viability to the franchise opportunity being offered. In reality, the market is much more effective at changing behaviour.

In franchising's case, this industry relied upon the confidence of that large sector of the business opportunity market called the Intrapreneurs. Being risk-adverse, they became very wary of franchising thus forcing the industry to evolve to deliver the individual success rates necessary to attract the Intrapreneurs.

> ## By increasing the success rate, it would be easier to recruit the right sort of franchisee, the Intrapreneur.

Two Key Innovations

To create the maximum success rates, franchisors introduced two key innovations into their franchise systems; revenue based fees and competence based training.

1. **Revenue based fees.** By changing the main proportion of franchise fees from joining fees to fees based on the franchisees revenues or customer sales, they created a win-win situation. High sales meant everyone made money. It also showed a commitment by the franchisor to the success of the franchisee.
2. **Competence based training.** Traditionally franchisee systems were not detailed and the franchisee was focused on creating performance immediately, even though they were technically incompetent. Intrapreneurs want certainty so the training systems evolved whereby the new franchisee was focused on becoming competent before focusing on performance. This approach had already been pioneered by the world's most successful franchise company, McDonalds.

The McDonalds Example

McDonalds Corp is recognised as the most successful ever franchising company. Fundamental to their success is what is known as the Hamburger University created in 1961. It was created because founder Ray Kroc understood that only education would provide the quality and confidence needed to guarantee success.

Even today, a McDonalds franchise will cost at least $250,000 AND you must have a proven background of business experience YET still you will not get a franchise until you have passed the McDonalds Training Programme. How long does it take? The answer from their website reads...

"The comprehensive world class training program can be as short as 9 months or as long as 24 months on a part time basis, approximately 20 hours a week. Some candidates who devote more time to the training program may be able to accomplish program objectives in as little as 9 months. The completion of the training program is not based on time but on mastering the skills necessary to operate great restaurants."

Just to own and run a burger restaurant, they expect you to invest 9 months full-time, or 2 years part-time, learning their systems. AND still success is not measured in time, it's measured in the mastery of skills, commonly known as Competence.

Franchising gets 'lucky'

There are two types of luck. One type is the Lottery type where winning is pure chance. Then there is what some people call 'luck' yet is just smart business. This is when **Opportunity meets Preparation.**

Over the 1970's and 1980's, the franchising industry made these key strategic changes and proved their ability to produce programmes with very high success rates [the Preparation]. All it needed was a flood of new Intrapreneurs and global changes provided these new people. As the Keynote Report on Franchising, 4th ed., 1991 stated;

'Business format franchising entered a dynamic new phase during the 1980's, mainly as a result of economic and political changes. In the early 1980's, the growth in unemployment created a vast pool of individuals all wishing to try out their entrepreneurial skills by setting up their own business.

The decline in the manufacturing sector has also led to a growing service-oriented economy which is conducive to business format franchising as it represents an <u>efficient and flexible distribution system for goods and services</u>.'

Franchising grew by 600% in 6 years

According to the book 'Franchising' by Hall & Dixon, 'A second period of rapid expansion in the franchising industry emerged in the early 1980's'. In the UK, annual Gross Turnover grew from £850 million in 1984 to £5,240 million in 1990. An incredible 600% growth! From this new growth boom came new companies such as The Body Shop.

Around the developed world, franchising entered the Growth Stage of its Lifecycle. This growth has continued to present day and now the statistics on the Franchising industry are incredible for an industry that was scorned and nearly banned in the 1970's. The USA market is a $1.5trillion industry and in Australia is over $120billion.

I like to refer to the UK market because it is a naturally conservative market yet even here, the industry still grows rapidly today growing 27% from 2005-2007 and is 15 times larger than 1984; over twenty years after it entered its Growth Stage.

The Secret

The secret to franchising's success is obvious: a low **failure** rate. When one compares it with other business opportunities, it is clear why the risk-adverse Intrapreneurs still flood into this industry.

The US Commerce Commission reports that 80% of new businesses close down after five years with 40% closing in the first year. This means that at least 50% of all businesses are closing, for whatever reason, each year. For those wishing to own their own business, the costs of business failure should never be under-estimated.

Compare this with the Franchise industry, where the industry associations report that total franchisee closures are less than 10% per year with countries such as the UK and Australia reporting percentages close to 5% annually. Franchising has over 500% higher success rates than normal businesses. All created by customer revenues and competence based training.

By increasing the success rate, it would be easier to recruit the right sort of franchisee, the Intrapreneur.

The Major Lessons

The lessons to be learnt from Franchising's history are:

1. <u>It takes Entrepreneurs to establish an industry.</u> Only entrepreneurs have the vision and courage to pioneer and establish industry. Entrepreneurs will also take the shortest route to making money so it was natural for them to eventually trying to succeed by focusing on recruiting new franchisees.

2. <u>Intrapreneurs dominate business opportunity seekers.</u> No-one cared that the Internet dot.com collapse meant that huge numbers of entrepreneurs and their investors lost money. The reason there was such public outcry to Franchising's failure rate was that it appealed to Intrapreneurs. Franchising proved that the bulk of business opportunity seekers are not entrepreneurs, they are risk-adverse Intrapreneurs.

3. <u>Intrapreneurs create booms.</u> The incredible growth boom in franchising over the past 20 years has proven that Intrapreneurs are a commercial force in society to be reckoned with. The key to harnessing the incredible power of the Intrapreneur is to create an environment where there is a high success rate.

4. <u>Intrapreneurs need competence training.</u> Intrapreneurs need the confidence gained through competence in a system to be motivated for success.

5. <u>Price is worth the Reward.</u> The evolution in Franchising systems created the opportunity for the boom in the 1980s when a flood of Intrapreneurs started looking for low risk opportunities.

How long is each stage in the lifecycle?

There is no answer to this, yet we know that technology lifecycles are getting shorter every year. Lifecycles based on other business concepts or products still are measured in decades as life doesn't change that quickly. The Growth Stage in Franchising is over 20 years old! Consequently, franchising is the major sector of business economies and still grows at rates other mature industries dream of!

Network Marketing

Birth Stage – 1940's to late 1970's

Network Marketing developed from the direct sales industry and, like most new marketing methods started in the USA.

In the 1940's, a company called Californian Vitamins first allowed its direct sales people to also recruit other sales people for a commission on their recruit's sales. Two of the top salesmen then formed the Amway Corporation, which has become the largest Network Marketing company in the world.

The greatest challenge to this business occurred in the late 1970s. As explained in the Franchising section, many Franchising companies focused purely on recruiting and many new franchisees failed losing large amounts of money. Few unscrupulous operators then applied the multi-level concept to this to create what became known as 'pyramid' franchise systems, or 'pyramid selling'.

After the government had attacked franchising, it then tried to ban the multi-level commission concept taking Amway to court. Amway fought for three years and won in 1979 thereby proving that multi-level commission concept of Network Marketing was a legally justifiable form of business.

Network Marketing had expanded in a few other countries yet the development was insignificant compared to what was happening in the United States.

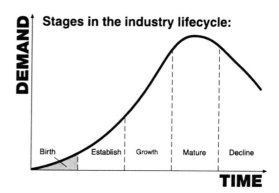

Stages in the industry lifecycle:

DEMAND

Birth   Establish   Growth   Mature   Decline

TIME

Birth Stage Points

1. Led by innovators - entrepreneurs

2. Pioneered in the USA

3. Impacted by franchise pyramid selling fight in 1970's

4. Proven in US courts as fair

5. Pioneering for 30 years

Establishment Stage – 1980s to 2000's

Amway's legal success started this industry's Establishment Stage initially in North America and then elsewhere. Like the Internet boom, from 1979 to 1984 hundreds of new companies were launched and the US Direct Selling Association reports that over 1 million people joined!

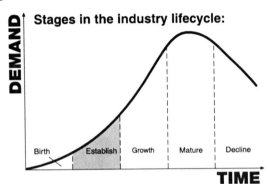

Stages in the industry lifecycle:

Over the following decade, every year saw the launch of new companies based on a new type of product or innovation in the Network Marketing business system. New forms of compensation plans were devised as were new forms of marketing or communications systems.

By the end of the 2000's, 15 million Americans were involved in Direct Sales, with most in Network Marketing. Sales had reached $30billion.

Worldwide

Although there were a few international pioneers, such as UK based, Kleeneze which introduced the first Network Marketing programme in Europe in 1970, the Birth Stage of Network Marketing was effectively in the USA. Following their US success, a group of Network Marketing companies then expanded internationally creating 'beachhead' booms in the other regions of the world in countries such as Brazil, UK, Australia, Taiwan and Japan.

Americas

Expansion into Central and South America, has been a natural focus for US companies. Millions flooded into companies in Brazil, Argentina, Colombia and Venezuela. Mexico was slower than other countries yet has expanded continuously, eventually matching Brazil and overtaking all other American markets. Maybe this woke the Brazilians up as their market boomed in the late 2000's.

Europe

Following their UK success, companies expanded across Europe targeting the major market of Germany then expanding into other Western European markets. With the end of the Cold War, companies expanded across Eastern Europe [Hungary, Poland] eventually starting a boom in Russia by the late 1990's. When the industry reached Russia, 1.5 million people joined in just 3 years. They say that there were even opportunity meetings in the Kremlin! (Lenin must be rolling in his grave.)

Each country in Europe has embraced Network Marketing in its own typical European style. Some markets have grown quickly and some great results have been produced by a number of companies. In other markets, companies have had to adjust significantly to local regulations and prejudices against entrepreneurs and new forms of business.

By the end of the 2000's, every country in Europe had an established Network Marketing industry with lessons learnt on how to grow a company in that market. Over nine million people were involved in the Direct salesindustry producing over US$27 billion in sales, most were in Network Marketing.

Asia

The Asian region has been the global success story. Following success in Japan, Taiwan, Australia and New Zealand, the lead companies rolled into South Korea, Hong Kong, Malaysia, Thailand, the Philippines and Indonesia.

It took until the early 2000s, for the massive markets of China and India to begin their Growth Stage. Given the initial results, these two countries should provide incredible growth over the coming decade.

In Asian markets, the expansion was explosive. This system of business suits the Asian culture and the results continue to be astounding. Across the region, thousands of local companies have started selling every product imaginable. The industry grew by a staggering 20 million people in just 20 years. Of the 12 countries where 1 million people are involved in each country, eight are Asian countries.

Africa and elsewhere

South Africa and Israel are strong, Nigeria is growing and companies are pioneering the less capitalist democratic countries of the world. Facts are difficult to discover yet every year there is another success story heard in countries such as Dubai, Morocco or Kenya.

Summary

The Establishment Stage finished in each country at different times. Some less developed countries are still being established.

The last 30 years has been the "MLM Era". The key innovation driving the industry was expansion by recruiting people into an MLM business opportunity.

Establishment Stage points:

- Led by entrepreneurs
- Every country and nearly every product concept has been pioneered
- A clear dominant business model has been pioneered
- A global trade association in the Direct Selling Association [DSA] under the World Federation of DSAs
- A core group of global companies with annual sales of at least a billion dollars
- A few billionaire company owners and thousands of Network Leaders are millionaires
- $100 billion in annual sales and millions of people involved
- Stabilising for 30 years

Independent Research

The PriceWaterhouseCoopers report on Direct Selling in Europe revealed that:
- Direct Selling provided work for more that 3.9 million full-time equivalent jobs.
- Accounted for over $40billion in annual revenues.
- The education standards were the same as the general public
- Over 90% of those Direct Sellers claim to be satisfied with their occupation (HOW MANY INDUSTRIES WOULD CLAIM THIS !)

A study conducted in the UK by the Westminster Business School revealed that
- 93% of customers said they would buy again from direct sales companies
- 88% of customers said they would recommend buying from a Direct Selling Organisation to their friends and family
- three main reasons for making a purchase via the Direct Selling channel are "product need and appeal", "convenience" and "value for money".

Human value of Network Marketing/Direct Sales

More inspiring on a human level was The 1999 Social and Economic Impact study of the NZ Direct Selling industry by Otago University which provides useful independent verification of the potential of this industry. Apart from calculating that its actual economic impact is **1500% greater than industry expenditure**, a survey of representatives confirmed why so many people are joining:

- 80.0% felt their lifestyle had improved
- 90.0% felt they had learnt new skills or improved old ones
- 93.0% agreed their communication skills had improved
- 87.5% felt more confident
- 85.5% felt more motivated
- 83.5% felt more independent
- 79.0% had a new direction in life

No other industry with mass numbers of people could claim to have this positive impact on the people involved!

The Next Stage?

The $64,000 question to ask is...

*'Will Network Marketing now enter its Growth Stage OR
has it actually already had this stage and is now becoming mature?'*

Those involved with the industry will immediately scoff at the thought of
'maturity' yet we have to investigate this to have 100% confidence in Network
Marketing's future. And this is not a new industry, it has been around for six
decades with millions involved producing tens of billions of dollars.

Obviously my positive language throughout this book shows that I think that
Network Marketing is entering its Growth Stage rather than Maturity and here
are the reasons why:

1. <u>Massive Growth Trends.</u> Our analysis of the Four Primary Trends proves
   that Network Marketing will be driven by these trends.

2. <u>Undeveloped Markets.</u> When analyzed on a percentage of population basis,
   there is enormous potential in all parts of the world, especially in key
   developing markets such as Latin America, China, India and Eastern Europe.
   Interestingly, one of the biggest potential growth regions is Western Europe
   as, unsurprisingly, it has been slower to embrace Network Marketing in its
   entrepreneurial stages.

3. <u>Substantial Productivity Potential.</u> Productivity is revenue per person
   involved and, with the new techniques being introduced it will be increased.
   Increases in productivity are the key to higher long term income and to
   increased success rates.

Powerful trends combined with barely tapped markets and rapidly increasing
productivity are the perfect conditions for a growth boom. They are certainly
NOT the conditions one sees in an industry approaching its Maturity Stage!

---

*There is the potential for Network Marketing to
grow by many times its current level*

Growth Stage – late 1990s onwards

It is always difficult to tell when one Stage of a Lifecycle stops and the next begins. When one looks globally, this is impossible as each country will be at a different stage in its Lifecycle.

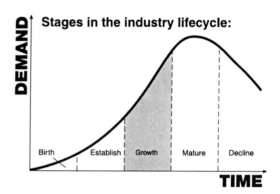

What happens is that companies evolve their businesses and new companies launch based on what they see as the 'Best Practice'. These are the indicators of strategic change. In Network Marketing from the late 1990s important developments emerged confirming the industry's strategic change. They were:

- **Customer Revenue.** Just as Franchising had done in the 1970's and employed the latest technology, companies focused on building customer revenues. If possible, they linked customers to company customer service departments.
- **Business Re-engineering.** All major companies undertook significant strategic development of their businesses covering everything from product ranges through to the promotion of new key management as the pioneering executives retired or took less arduous roles.
- **Classic Direct Sales introduced MLM.** The bulk of the classic Single Level Direct Sales companies began introducing Network Leadership Programmes, including Avon, the industry's largest company.

Combined these were the most significant changes in Network Marketing for decades. They are a clear indication of an industry in fundamental strategic change and signify the entry into a new Stage of development.

> *from the late 1990s, important developments emerged confirming the industry's strategic change*

New Boom

In the 2000s, the new growth strategies implemented by companies were showing results are fantastic as the sales graph from the World Federation of Direct Selling Association [WFDSA] show.

<u>Retail Sales</u> – the actual sales clearly show the boom until end of the 1990's, the period of consolidation [with a small decline], then the start of this new boom. From 2001-2008, over 35% growth!

Estimated Global Retail Sales
2001-2006 over 39% growth
Billions of U.S. Dollars
(As of December 2006)

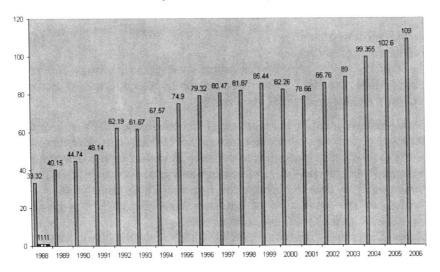

In conclusion Network Marketing has all of the key elements to show it is entering its Growth Stage; global success, established companies, large growth potential, a strong trade association and a new strategy for expansion yet something seems missing...

Tipping Point

All the strategic developments mentioned are positively impacting growth in an exciting way yet there is still something missing to push the growth of this industry past its **Tipping Point** into momentum in the Growth Stage.

I will explain what is that **Missing Link** [as some leaders have called it], that one new innovation, that will push this industry over its Tipping Point and into a new boom. I predict that this one innovation will make the biggest impact on the development of this industry since the original MLM concept pioneered 60 years ago.

When you can appreciate the impact of this innovation then you will understand why I am more excited about the future of Network Marketing today than I have been in 20 years. Why I think you should have **100% Confidence.**

What's the Tipping Point?

The concept of the 'Tipping Point' was made famous by the international bestselling book by Malcolm Gladwell of the same name. A Tipping Point is the point in a Stage of each Lifecycle after which growth [or decline] accelerates. When momentum is created.

The beginning of the Growth Stage of Network Marketing was actually a few years ago. Some companies began using these next generation strategies in the late 1990s. We have started to see the results over the past few years and now we are ready for that final innovation to push this industry over its Tipping Point and into momentum, sometimes known as hyper-growth!

The Franchising industry introduced the new developments during the late 1970's and early 1980s entering the Growth Stage of its Lifecycle. By the early 1980's, the industry had proven its success system and a flood of new Intrapreneurs joined pushing growth past its Tipping Point. Growth suddenly exploded. In the UK, it grew by 600% in just 5 years.

The Missing Link

The innovation in Network Marketing that will push Network Marketing past its Tipping Point into a new explosive growth period is the same as Franchising; **competence based training.**

What is this?

I am sure you know what competence based training is, even if you don't recognize the words. It is the standard education, training and personnel development strategy in every school, organisation and military in the world.

The concept is simple. You work out what you need to know or be able to do [known as competencies] and then you set 'competence' standards to prove you have mastered them.

Competence based training is used for every position where you can define what is needed for success and a minimum achievement level. This becomes the foundation for that position and everyone is expected to focus on becoming competent BEFORE they focus on their performance for results.

Look how important competence is to success:

- Competence is the **basis for confidence.** You can never expect to have high confidence levels if you were not competent [i.e. incompetent].

- Competence is the **basis for motivation** because confidence is the key to releasing motivation. You can be highly motivated yet this will die with low confidence.

- Competence is the **basis for productivity.** Only competent and confident people can be expected to produce satisfactory levels of performance.

- Competence is the **basis for individual success**. The team performance may be great yet only competence can deliver the basis for individual performance.

What's happened?

At this point in this discussion, I find that some people are shaking their heads and wondering why the Network Marketing industry has not implemented competence based training before. It seems so logical, what has happened?

Franchising's journey

The first point I would make is that Franchising did not implement competence based training as the foundation for the franchise system until the 1980s. Network Marketing's journey has mirrored theirs.

Pioneer and Establishment Stage

In these early stages of the Franchise industry's life, the focus of the industry was 'growth at all costs' as this business was so new. Opportunities seemed unlimited. And the public had no experience of this form of business. This industry was naturally dominated by entrepreneurs all looking to get rich from this concept.

There was no 'best practice' to follow so entrepreneurs did whatever they thought was the best way to create success as fast as possible. And the fastest way was to sell Franchise Systems and to support this, entrepreneurs wanted their new franchisees to create sales quickly to 'prove' the system works. This Performance First Strategy with a Franchise

> **Franchise System**
> **Performance First**

system works for a few yet most will fail without learning the skills or having the support of other successful people. Thus eventually the failure rate balloons and a company dies. As an industry, it took until the 1970s for the failure rate to become such a problem that franchising was forced to change.

The innovation that changed the productivity, profitability, confidence was competence based training; pioneered by McDonalds since 1962. This one innovation exploded the success rates so the industry appealed to Intrapreneurs. Franchising passed the Tipping Point and boomed in the 1980s.

> **Franchise System**
> **Competence First**

The Door-knocking Legacy

Other than the entrepreneurs dominating our industry's early growth, the second reason that competence based training is only now being implemented in the Direct Sales/Network Marketing industry is more fundamental to our history. It is also the reason why some of the older leaders struggle with this new strategy.

We sometimes forget that Network Marketing wasn't a totally new business; it evolved from the classic forms of Direct Sales, such as door knocking.

Therefore it is logical that whatever the philosophies were in developing a door-knocking team this was the basis for developing a Network [even though they are totally different concepts]. So let's look at the core philosophies in Door Knocking.

- **Most people will fail.** People have to sell to people they don't know so there is a lot of 'rejection' felt. The rejection is a nightmare for most people so most people quit in days or weeks. NOTHING will change this.
- **Attitude and motivation are key.** The skills required are low so your attitude and motivation to keep working in the face of rejection is the key to success.
- **Success is in numbers.** Some people will buy and some will not. The key to success is to just keep knocking doors and eventually you will succeed.

Based on these sales person realities, what are the Leader Success strategies?
- **Action NOW.** Sales people quit quickly so get them working IMMEDIATELY.
- **Create RAPID RESULTS.** Sales people have no commitment, low confidence and big rejection so only rapid results will keep them working.
- **Training = Motivation.** As people don't last, what is called 'training' becomes mass motivational events rather than individual skills based coaching.
- **Success is a Recruiting Game.** Most sales people fail quickly so Leaders must focus on Recruiting. We call this approach the 'Recruiting Game'.

The core strategy is PERFORMANCE first and never competence.

Time to evolve

Anyone experienced in Network Marketing will recognize that the philosophies used in classic Direct Sales became the core philosophies in our business. This was only natural YET given that the industry has had to recruit and motivate entrepreneurs; it was probably the correct strategy to use. A US$100bil global industry is proof.

The fact is that it is not the correct strategy now. The reasons are simple:

- **Franchise system not Direct Seller.** The fact is that a Network business opportunity is not a direct sales opportunity so the core development strategies are different. It is a franchised business opportunity and for the same reasons as Franchising, the foundation of the system should be competence.

- **Skills can be learnt.** Network Marketing is based on **three core skills** and as everyone can learn the skills [to competence], everyone can create success. This is why this approach is known as 100% Success.

100% SUCCESS

- **No cold selling.** Network Marketing operates in the warm market of people's friends, family and associates. You should never 'sell' to or pressure your warm market thus successful recruiting is based on the confidence you have that the person will succeed. This ONLY comes from a competence based programme.

- **Few people join with the confidence** to take massive action at the start. The lack of confidence undermines their motivation guaranteeing failure. The ONLY way to build confidence and motivation is through a focus on learning skills first.

Network System

Competence

Guaranteed Success!

A Network Marketing business based on COMPETENCE BEFORE PERFORMANCE, means that everyone has a 100% Chance of success. It means we have confidence in offering that 'guaranteed success' one gets from Franchising.

Simple Evolution

Changing from a Performance First to a Competence First approach is a relatively quick process. Important points to note:

- **The 'System' does not change.** The 'Learning' part of the Business System is upgraded and expanded.

- **Upline system does not change.** If you have no experience in Network Marketing you will not know of an amazing support concept that makes this business 10 times better than Franchising for the new Intrapreneur. It's called the **Upline system.** In Network Marketing, new people are trained [coached] by successful leaders [Upline] and they are paid by a commission on your sales.

> **Your System**
> Learning System

Thus your coaches have the best experience and financial motivation to help you. The competence approach makes this Upline system work much more effectively for the new person.

Guaranteed Success

The last point you need to know about the competence approach in Network Marketing is about I call 'The Knowledge™'. And this is only for those currently involved or thinking of joining.

In the old days of Network Marketing, we just sent people out to work as soon as they joined. This was how we were trained and there was no requirement to learn any basic theory of how to build a network. The 'Basics' were obvious, join, use product, talk to people. Recruit numbers until you found someone who could produce some results.

> **Learning System**
> The Knowledge™

The future is about Quality, not quantity. With competence approach everyone can succeed which means everyone must 'learn'. So FIRST they must learn what the BASIC THEORY upon which every System is based. It's like an operating manual. It's NOT optional, you must learn this theory or you will NEVER be able to operate a Network System properly.

What is exciting is that everyone can learn quickly, the 'Knowledge' is the same for all companies and can be learnt through new online elearning courses. By learning the knowledge, you will learn the skills of the system properly which means you have a 100% chance of success. **Success will be guaranteed.** My version is on **www.100percentknowledge.com**, have a look.

Key Growth Factors

To see whether the timing is right for the Growth Boom, we lastly need to investigate in relation to the Key Growth Factors that promoted the boom in Franchising (Network Marketing's nearest relation). From 'Franchising' by Hall & Dixon, the five critical growth factors finally came in place:

1. It had spent time as a 'fringe' form of business, building its reputation as its successful companies fine-tuned their systems to the culture.

2. It had a sufficient number of successful companies to expand from.

3. It had a strengthening regulatory environment, including a strong trade association in the British Franchise Association.

4. It was developing an increasingly positive media image.

5. It had huge success overseas to measure against.

Growth Factor 1 Successful systems

As stated earlier, all good Network Marketing companies have recently rationalized their complete programmes to make them more productive, effective and successful. The introduction of the new 100% Success Competence strategies mean everyone who joins [like Franchising] can be successful.

The only true measure of a successful business system is durability. In every country of the world, there are a number of local and foreign companies, which are **'local adapted'** and these companies are growing year on year. They are achieving activity and productivity levels of which the pioneering companies could only have dreamed.

Growth Factor 2 Sufficient company numbers

One company on its own does not make an industry and all industries have proved that you need a small group to create the momentum necessary to create true growth and excitement. There are no standard measures with many companies with hundreds of millions or billion dollar turnover, this required number has been achieved.

Growth Factor 3 Strong Regulatory Environment

A strong regulatory environment is required by any industry so that unlawful operators can be prosecuted and consumers and junior participants protected. Government legislation combats unethical operators on the fringes of the industry and trade associations regulate those operating in the main stream. Governments cannot effectively protect consumers or junior participants, as has been shown in countless industries such as insurance and financial services. Industries must police themselves.

There are very strong laws governing Network Marketing in most countries. They protect the consumer and the new entrant. The Direct Selling Association is active in all countries directing the industry.

Growth Factor 4 Positive media image

Positive media coverage is difficult for all industries that do not have a large advertising budget. The media profile of Network Marketing is similar to the level when Franchising began its boom in the 1980s.

As a reaction to the unethical conduct of companies in earlier years and Network Marketing companies now *pride themselves on their level of ethics.* Their success in this area has caused press coverage to improve.

As the continued improving success rates filter throughout society, it is expected that the media coverage will continue to improve just as it did with franchising.

Growth Factor 5 Overseas Success

Wherever you live, you can look overseas to incredible success. There are 15 countries with over $1billion in sales and five more that should breach this milestone within five years. There are 12 more countries with more than 1 million people involved and four more that should breach this milestone within five years.

The important point to accept is that the success in not centred in one specific region or one culture. Every region has success stories. Every country has success stories. It has boomed in Christian, Muslim, Buddhist, Hindu, Jewish and Taoist cultures. Rich, poor and developing countries.

> ## *All five growth factors are in place today*

One Last Massive Push

Even though we did not need this, the economic meltdown starting in 2008 is a massive opportunity for the network marketing industry. The number of people looking for or wanting a great part-time income or full-time business is rocketing. This is like a massive push to help us boom.

Ironically, the last time there was such high levels of unemployment and financial insecurity was in the 1980s which, as the 1991 Keynote Report of Franchising drove Franchising into its NEW BOOM as it *created a vast pool of individuals all wishing to try out their entrepreneurial skills by setting up their own business*.

Summary

Here is a summary of the facts:

- The Direct Sales industry rises or falls based on the Network Marketing sector which accounts for over 95% of the business.

- All the evidence supports the prediction that Network Marketing has entered the Growth Stage of its Lifecycle. This should be the largest Stage of growth in the industry history and should last at least two decades.

- The key strategic developments have already been made at corporate level. The last innovation needed to push the industry past the Tipping Point into explosive growth is the introduction of competence based training and this is now happening.

- The only credible comparable business would be Franchising and the developments within Network Marketing mirror their history.

So there you are. I think the evidence is so overwhelming you should have 100% Confidence that this industry truly is the **Right Place at the Right Time**. This opportunity is not for everyone yet for most people it is the best opportunity for them. Will you take this opportunity? I will refer to the wisdom of Winston Churchill who said

'Men [and women] occasionally stumble over the truth, but most pick themselves up and hurry off as if nothing has happened.'

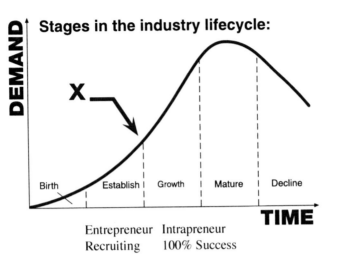

Stages in the industry lifecycle:

Birth | Establish | Growth | Mature | Decline

Entrepreneur   Intrapreneur
Recruiting   100% Success

Network Marketing Life Cycle

Nothing could be simpler than the Lifecycle graph of Network Marketing above. The past was driven by entrepreneurs offering the excitement of NEW opportunities! It created growth yet low success rates.

Today we are at the point X. The future is one of exciting growth driven by Intrapreneurs offering a proven opportunity with a 100% chance of success if you focus on Competence First.

Predictions for the Future

In 1999, a friend of mine sat next to a leading executive in Vodafone, then the world's largest mobile telecommunications company. He asked him, whether in the early 1990's they predicted the explosive growth in the mobile industry?

The executive smiled and said that they had predicted very strong growth yet, in relationship to what actually happened, they would be embarrassed to show people how low they were in their estimations!

My next-door neighbour was a leading sales manager in Compaq in the late 1980's as the PC industry went crazy in its Growth Stage – every year she sold 100% above her budget. Who in the UK franchising industry at the start of the 1980's would have predicted 600% growth in that decade?

When we look at the Growth Stage in all industry Lifecycles, the growth actually created was always substantially higher than anyone could have credibility predicted at the start. For this reason I am going to be short and general in predictions.

- **Growth Drivers.** The key drivers of global growth will be the productivity revolution and continued boom in the developing regions from South America to Eastern Europe, especially the BRIC countries [Brazil, Russia, India and China].

- **Sales Predictions.** Direct Sales industry will grow from approximately US$100billion to $200billion by 2018. The same growth in 10 years than the previous 60 years to create.

- **Numbers involved.** In the past, I focused on predicting the growth in numbers of people involved as the core growth strategy was based on recruiting new people. The future should see numbers continued to increase yet at a much slower rate as sales. This is a very positive sign as it means productivity [and incomes] is increasing!

100% CONFIDENCE
Regional Growth

Asia Pacific

This has been the shining star of Network Marketing recently. From New Zealand to Japan, the industry has boomed [and continues to grow]. Obviously China and India are going to be exciting markets, though the more established markets of Korea, Taiwan, Thailand and Malaysia continue to excite people with their results. Australia, New Zealand and Singapore are expected to follow Japan's lead the productivity stakes.

The Americas

All eyes are on the USA as it is the bellwether market and home to most of the global companies as they determine the speed of change globally. Whilst the competence training innovation was not developed in the USA, the Americans are amazing in the way they can embrace new ideas and roll them out on a global scale.

South America has an industry much larger than people imagine and Brazil is continuing to be the major driving force down there. Mexico has delivered huge results. There is currently exciting growth in every country and there is no reason why this will slow down in the future.

Europe

This has been the most conservative region for growth as one would expect. The large number of countries, languages, cultures and regulations often led people into the belief that it is a difficult market to develop. The natural European negativity often leads people to believe that they are not entrepreneurial or interested in new business ideas. These are totally incorrect assumptions, as the facts prove. Network Marketing is booming across the region with [at printing] at least 17 countries showing growth!

I have worked across Europe in this business for nearly two decades and I expect Europe to benefit more from a productivity focus more than any other region. High productivity means high success rates and Europeans has a cultural terror of failure developed over centuries. The Europeans are expected to lead the productivity revolution in Network Marketing.

Middle East and Africa

The Middle East has been slowly developing and Israel, in particular, has produced great results. Africa is now developing in many countries and, as expected, South Africa leading the way.

Women Dominate Leadership

Women already dominate the Network Marketing industry in terms number of people involved and the percentage is growing. This trend is expected to continue and, with the change of focus from recruiting to competence coaching, they are expected dominate the next generation of leadership.

The Big Get Bigger

Large companies always dominate an industry and Network Marketing is no different as 100 companies produce at least 50% of all global sales. Their proportion of the industry is expected to grow as a 'productivity focus' is more effective recruiting message when backed by a large company.

Summary

There will be further growth of $100billion within ten years and there will be explosive growth in every country and region of the world. I do not know how to put this more bluntly, now is the best time to join the Network Marketing industry in the past 60 years and for the next 20 years.

*NOW is the best time to join the Network Marketing industry
in the past 60 years and for the next 20 years*

If this all sounds too good to be true then heed the following warnings:

- You must be involved in the 'Right Company' and follow their Success System closely. Take The Knowledge to ensure you are guaranteed of success. This is how fortunes are created.
- Expect change. If an organisation is not innovating and changing with the market, then it will die. Do not resist change, celebrate it.

POINT: If you are one of the million people who have joined and left a Network Marketing opportunity over the past ten years, now is the time to rejoin. Take advantage of the knowledge and skills you learned

The Major Benefit

So far all we've discussed are economics, logic, numbers and money. The reason for life is to feel good about yourself and others. The major benefit of Network Marketing is by far the Personal Growth element and Relationship gains. It is a particular focus of the industry and a major attraction to its participants.

If we could replace most people's income from their current job and give them the FREEDOM to earn more if they wanted to, work from home, spend more quality time with their family, increase their social life, reduce their stress, increase their travel and feel better about themselves, everyone would consider joining. Not by *promising more money*, just by giving them the chance to enjoy their life with what they've got. Most people don't care about earning great fortunes, they're more interested in enjoying life.

The personal development side of Networking is my favourite area, as we see so many people, especially women, gain in confidence and self esteem. People gain the strength to make decisions which improve their lifestyle and those living around them. No other industry does this on the scale of Network Marketing.

As a person's belief in themself grows, they change for the better and I've been privileged to see so much of this. Many people fear growth and what others may think. To them I say that everyone deserves to feel better about themself and our business is based on doing just that.

The Right Business

There are essentially two messages in this book. Firstly that Network Marketing has entered its Growth Stage so it is a great industry to join today. The second message is that it is essential that you join the right company because only few companies will succeed in this new growth stage. So how do you pick or know you are with, the right company?

This is a tough question because nothing in business is guaranteed. The best you can do is to reduce the odds of failure by ensuring the following key points are in place:

- **Look for strategy.** The basic strategy of the company must be simple and obvious. You do not need to do a lot of research, it must immediately seem correct.

- **Look for leadership.** After strategy, leadership is the next most important key to success. There must be proven, competent leadership. Success is based on clear leadership skills today.

- **Look for strength.** The key to the right business may not be its size, its strength of the business. A company that dominates a specific product area has big opportunities to grow rather than one which is a copy of a successful business claiming to have more growth opportunities. Due to this selling method, the potential market for all products is huge, the key is the business behind it.

- **Join a successful team.** Strong companies have the resources to succeed in the new market. The power to compete against the retail stores. The power to invest in the latest technology. They have the success stories to appeal to strong people longing for a long term opportunity.

- **Look for a customer focus.** Network marketing has pioneered the best systems to grow a company. There may be a few new innovations in systems yet they are unlikely to have huge impact. Long term success is more based on a business's ability to find and keep customers. Look for this customer focus.

- **Look for clear rewards at all levels.** An organisation with all leaders and no workers will always fail. An organisation with all workers and no leaders will never grow. An organisation must offer an opportunity for both types of people and the rewards must reflect the different effort invested.

Your Challenge

Carpe Diem - Seize the Day.

My challenge to you is to invest some more time in your future. I do not know at what stage in your life this book has reached you. What I guarantee you is that the world you live in is changing at a pace few realise and you are perfectly placed to take advantage of this. I implore you to examine and re-read the theory to decide its relevance to you.

The Magic Formula of success is simple: *Right place at the Right Time with the Right Business.* If the factors are in place, people make fortunes and the average person can make an above-average income compared to efforts in another business.

Lifestyle will be the focus of the 2000s. Those who can supply a *self employed income* to the average person to improve their rapidly decreasing lifestyle will be in the Business of the 2000s. The concept of the *'People's Franchise'* is something for everyone. Against other forms of Self-Employed incomes, it offers the greatest rewards for the least risk with the best chance of enjoying your lifestyle. It suits the Intrapeneur Business Opportunity Seekers who are the powerhouse of the self employed sector.

The Direct Shopping sector of the distribution of consumer goods offers the greatest area of business potential. Network Marketing is the method of distribution best structured to satisfy both consumer and manufacturer. The confused consumer is searching for people who will make life simpler and more exciting. They want to be inspired and Network Marketing is best placed to provide this.

Four Primary Trends are behind Network Marketing ensuring it will continue to be a Growth industry and *The Right Place* for many people, if only on a part-time basis.

The *Establish Stage of an Industry Lifecycle* is the pioneer stage known for exciting products, ideas and success stories. It is also recognised for high failure rates and a poor public image. This was the experience of PC, mobile, Internet and franchising. Success is achieved and Network Marketing pioneered 100 countries and created $100billion in sales with 50 million people involved.

The *Growth Stage* is the 'money-making' period of an industry's history. The industry mindset changes from excitement from 'potential' to 'proven' results. Those strong companies with the right strategy dominate and lead the greatest period of expansion. This is the period when companies like Nokia, Microsoft and Google became global giants.

All the elements for Network Marketing are in place for the Growth Stage, including those *five critical Growth Factors* franchising has needed to boom. It is not surprising that the industry has growth in nearly every country in the world. $100billion increase in sales over 10 years is more than possible, it is probably too conservative. The *timing is right* to become involved now.

Our theory is that there is a revolution in society that is refocusing life on the rewards of an increased *lifestyle*. This can only be universally provided by a stable income, unlikely to come from the employment sector.

If you are a new distributor in Network Marketing, we trust we have increased your *feeling of certainty* about your business. If you ever want to quit to take other Self-Employed income opportunities or a job, we hope you now realise that you are probably leaving the best opportunity around for more dangerous waters. Not the best decision for the informed, wouldn't you agree?

The major benefit of involvement in Network Marketing is the *personal growth people achieve*. The money's great but life is more about how you feel about yourself than how much money you have. We have seen no other industry improve the self-esteem and self-worth of people as Network Marketing.

We thank you for taking the time to invest in yourself and hope these theories will strike a chord of logic as well as an emotional desire to have, do and be more in your life. Network Marketing offers you a business that is simple, it works and anyone can do it. And millions will.

It is important to follow your 'truth' in life. Be careful about accepting the opinions of others until the facts around a specific question stack up in your mind. I openly admit that I did not feel comfortable with this industry until I did some research into its potential; so I understand if you have some reservations. Inevitably there will be some people who do not embrace this opportunity based on lack of understanding, often criticising without justification. To them I offer the words of the great philosopher Cicero who said,

'They condemn what they do not understand'

For the sceptics......

"Radio has no future"
Lord Kelvin, Scottish mathematician and physicist 1897

"Television won't be able to hold on to any market after the first six months. People will soon get tired of staring at a plywood box every night."
Darryl F Zanuck, Head of 20th Century Fox 1946

"We don't like their sound. Groups of guitars are on the way out."
Decca Records rejecting the Beatles 1962

Extra Points for Discussion that people ask about or need to know

Understanding Pyramid Selling

'The truth shall set you free'

Often people confuse Network Marketing with a concept called 'Pyramid Selling', questioning whether it is legal or not.

Distributors and members of the public all over the world are plagued by this phantom beast called 'Pyramid Selling'. It is also a tool used by sceptical and uninspiring pessimists to attack less confident distributors. It is time to kill this beast for good.

The facts are:

- The term Pyramid Selling is coined when the majority of income for the company is made from the money people invest when they join, rather than from product sales. Companies that employ this Strategy are no more than recruiting schemes where for every winner there is a loser. Customers are the only people who can introduce profit into a business and make it legitimate.

- Franchising was originally called Pyramid Selling because companies made their money based on people joining rather than customer sales so many people failed, losing their investment in the process. The British Franchise Association was created primarily to try to disassociate reputable franchisors from pyramid selling operations which had proliferated in the late 1960's and early 1970's.

A pyramid scheme is simple to detect. You do this by looking at the product and by asking yourself whether it offers real value and excitement to a set customer target market? If it does not and customer sales are unlikely then the scheme will eventually be totally focussed on recruiting people and is, therefore, a pyramid.

In reality, the public is now alert to pyramid schemes so rarely last more than a few months.

NETWORK MARKETING WILL NOT SATURATE!

So many people ask if Network Marketing will saturate. No, it will not. The main reasons are:

1. There is a constant turnover of customers and distributors which ensures a steady and large supply of potential people.
2. Hundreds of thousands of 17 year olds turn 18 adding new potential distributors. People's circumstances change, making them more interested in a new opportunity.
3. Nearly all Network Marketing companies eventually offer international business opportunities dramatically expanding the potential market.
4. Companies are always looking to adjust and expand their product ranges increasing the potential market for their products.

NOTE: It is pertinent to point out that no product has ever saturated a market. Millions of TV sets are sold every year even though over 95% of houses already have sets.

Maturity Stage

Many people ask what happens when Network Marketing reaches its Maturity Stage. This is a fair question yet it must be accepted that this is more than 10 years away so it should have no impact on what you do and think today.

Purely for interest's sake, It is pertinent to note that when an industry reaches Maturity it normally undergoes a further round of competition. The end result is that a few large players remain dominating a product or distribution sector. The implications for Networkers will have little impact as these changes are at the company ownership level. What is real is that the growth opportunities are reduced yet the chances of success are high for the professional people. Much like the real estate industry is today.

Do I have to sell?

This is a common question even if not asked. The answer is 'No, you do not have to sell' if you think 'selling' means 'to pressure someone into buying from you. As Networkers we market our products through people we know and putting pressure on them breaks the trust upon which all strong relationships are built.

If 'selling' means asking people to buy a product that they want and making a profit, then 'Yes, you do sell.'

This can be an emotional issue and a significant block to people so it's best to know the facts.

- 95% of people do not like selling or believe they cannot sell. If the 95% look at a Network Opportunity and see a 'sales' business they may not be interested. They will say in their head 'I can't sell!'
- People do not want to 'sell' to their friends and family YET everyone is excited about telling someone about a product or service they believe in and think another person may want. This is called 'word-of-mouth' recommendation and is the foundation stone of Network Marketing.
- Network Marketing is a distribution business where its power is Sales and Marketing. We talk of 'selling products to customers' so it can easily look like a 'Sales' business. Be wary of any company that DOES NOT talk of selling products to customers [it is probably a pyramid!]

Inspirational Sales

There are two types of sales:

- **Professional Sales.** Professional sales people sell products to customers. This is their career and they develop high levels of sales skills. They will if need be apply pressure to the customer to gain the sale.
- **Inspirational Sales.** Sales made by non-professional sales. The customer buys the product based on the product strengths and the 'inspiration' provided by the promoter. The promoter has low sales skills. No pressure is applied.

Network Marketing companies use inspirational sales systems. This is the same sales as someone dealing with customers at a butcher, medical clinic, bank or restaurant. No pressure, the customer is in control. As long as the product is promoted with enthusiasm, satisfies a need and is good value, then customers will buy it and anyone can make money from it.

Get Rich Fast Schemes

Network Marketing is sometimes erroneously called a 'Get Rich Fast' scheme in a way that we should be embarrassed about. They use the title to infer it is illegal, immoral or the claims are unbelievable.

Whilst the illegal or immoral inferences are neither correct or humorous, the funny thing is that in some ways it is a 'Get Rich Fast' scheme! Compared to other methods of creating wealth, the average person can earn more money faster with a Network Marketing business, so it can justifiably, honestly and ethically be classified a Get Rich Fast scheme. This is a fact we should be proud of.

Let's compare Network Marketing

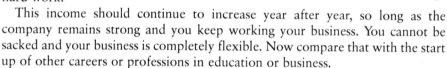

Income statisticians classify 'The Rich' as the top 20% of income earners, who earned an average of US$60,000 per year. In my experience of many Network Marketing companies, it should take between 3 to 7 years of hard work with a good solid company to be earning a $60,000 income per year. Note, I said HARD WORK. No-one joins the ranks of 'The Rich' without hard work.

This income should continue to increase year after year, so long as the company remains strong and you keep working your business. You cannot be sacked and your business is completely flexible. Now compare that with the start up of other careers or professions in education or business.

After 40 years of work, only 4% of people are financially secure. If it took 3 years, 5 years or even 7 years to reach this, then this opportunity offers a 'Get Rich Fast' scheme when compared to other income earning situations.

Government Recognised high earnings

The Direct Selling Association of the USA confirmed the high earnings available to people involved with direct sales with their 1992 USA government recognised survey. It showed that 50% of full-time direct sales people earned over $50,000 per year.

(note that less than 10% of people work full-time)

It also revealed that an astonishing 10% of full-time people earned over $100,000, per year. If $60,000 annual income is 'Rich', name another industry where anyone who really wants to succeed has a 1 in 10 chance of making the ranks of the 'Rich'.

The Real Power of Network Marketing

'I'd rather earn 1% of 100 people's efforts than 100% of my own'
Billionaire John Paul Getty

Everybody wants to know how much money you can earn in any business or job. If you go for a job interview, the most important questions normally are: *How much am I going to make?* and *What do I have to do to make it?*

In Network Marketing, it's very simple. You buy the company's products at a discounted wholesale price and sell them on at a higher retail price for a *Retail Profit.*

The company also allows you to sponsor new distributors and they (the company) will pay you a percentage of the price that the new distributors, and their teams, pay for their purchases. This is the company's cost of growth, or to look at it another way, their advertising and personnel development expenditure being spent in a different way. Instead of having to do all of the recruiting, interviewing, training and managing people; they pay you, the distributor, to do that for what should be called *'Leadership Bonuses'.*

Highly motivated people are vital to any 'people'-based business and nothing is more true in this business. They are the reason why Network Marketing companies can grow so quickly. Knowing *'how'* the money is made does not explain 'why' so many people become so highly motivated to join and succeed. Nor does it reveal its real power.

Including this section was a priority because few people really understand how this financial element gives Network Marketing its real power. Every Networker needs to understand where the real financial muscle is in this business and why it appeals to all income aspirations, especially to the people who only want a small part-time income.

90% of all people who join Networking are looking for a long term part-time income that will provide them with $100-300 extra per month. For some people, this does not sound a lot of money but it's only because you probably don't understand how this amount of money can radically change someone's life. Read on........

What do you think is the average household income?
$20,000? $40,000? Shall we say $30,000?
  (this is probably a little high for many areas)
So what is the monthly income? $2,500
The weekly income? $600 is close enough.

What percentage of that $600 does the average household spend on basic living expenses like... house, food, basic clothes, lights, gas, telephone, etc.
50%? 100%? (In seminars, many people yell out 110%).
Lets settle on 90%.
Is that fair? A bit high or a bit low, it doesn't really matter.

From this we can deduce that 10% of $600 or $60 a week is left over for people to spend on the finer more enjoyable things in life. Only $60 per week or $240 per month!
It's not much, is it?
This money is called disposable income or spending money. I call it Lifestyle money. It's the money with which people have fun. With it, they buy holidays, luxuries, meals out, etc.

The Real Power of Network Marketing is that the average person with part-time effort can earn $240 in one to three months of joining. Yes, they can Double their Lifestyle.

Obviously, the vast majority of people would love to earn more money and this is possible. Some part-time people earn as much as $5,000 per month but only after a long period of time or some luck in sponsoring. (Some would say 'good management!')

People on the 'part-time' Lifestyle plan also are involved with Network Marketing because of other benefits such as the improvement in confidence, new friendships, involvement with a new positive community and the recognition they receive.

Most of the money people will earn at this level is from retailing. This is why retailing must be actively encouraged in any company. An excess focus on leadership, big royalties and team building to the detriment of retail profits will scare away the Lifestyle Plan people, reducing the possible royalties for the 'leaders'.

Geometric Power of Numbers

Many people struggle with the idea of how they can earn a fortune from a few people – how does this exponential curve work? The answer is in the Geometric power of numbers.

One day an Indian prince was inspecting his lands when he came across a peasant playing chess.
Thinking he could not lose, the prince challenged the peasant to a game and arrogantly stated 'Defeat me and I'll give you whatever you want'
They started playing and, as normal in stories, there was an upset result and the peasant won. The prince says 'what do you want?' and, expecting to lose lands, animals or money, the peasant asked for rice.
'Put one grain of rice on the first square of this chess board. On the second put two grains, in the third put four grains. Double the grains for each square of the board' says the peasant.
The prince laughed and readily agrees, because being royal and this being a parable, he was stupid.
He orders his Rice Keeper to put the rice on the board. Only to find he is ruined. There are 64 squares on a chess board and if you double a grain of rice 63 times you end up with more rice than in all of India [nine billion billion grains!]

In Network Marketing, the Geometric Power of Numbers allows you to introduce a few people, help them learn the key skills in the company success system which will mean more people will join. You coach those new people to learn the system and more people join and so on. Eventually, the Power of Numbers will start to rapidly grow your network.

The peasant in the example only used two as the base number. If he used three x three x three or four x four x four, the numbers become enormous much faster.

The Glory of Residual Incomes

Eventually, your network will be too big for you to personally help individuals. Yet because everyone is using the same system, the network can continue to grow. If people are working independently of you, you have created a residual income – the ultimate in wealth creation. Your network has changed from a 'business' that needs action to an 'asset' like property, that makes money without further effort.

How an income grows

It is important that anyone involved with Network Marketing understands and appreciates the time it takes to develop a network and how the income grows.

A strong Network Marketing income develops in what is called an exponential curve. Understanding this curve is probably the most important thing you can learn in the first three months of your Network Marketing career.

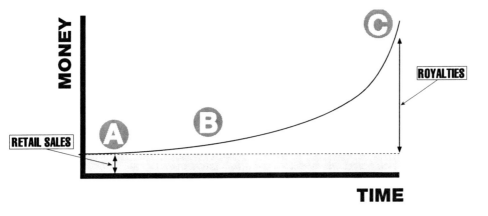

The Exponential Income Curve

The exponential curve shows that, in the beginning, income is small just like all careers and businesses. Money is made mainly from Retail sales. (Wholesale commissions are earned in some companies but they must be considered as repayment for your investment of time, money and effort in the recruitment and business building.)

If you are continually working in the correct manner, your team will grow and you will then be earning royalties. As your team continues to grow it will do so exponentially and so will your income.

Unfortunately you must put in the hard work at the start and you will see few results. For this reason, many people leave at point B because they expected results too fast. People would never quit at B if they believed they would be receiving the income achieved from Royalties by point C.

Avoiding poverty

It would be wrong to discuss income creation without briefly discussing what people do with their income and the concept of financial security. This is a subject few understand yet everyone knows how important it is to live a happy, secure and successful life.

The unfortunate facts are that by the time we reach 65 years old, only 4% of the population are financially secure. Everyone else will be either dead or dead broke.

'Broke' means that you need to rely on charity or government income support to survive. You are not in control of your financial situation and will suffer as the aging population squeezes most economies for money.

In fact, statistics show that the average 'retirement' income of the over 65 year olds is normally half the level of average national incomes. With the current cost of living and aging population, this means <u>poverty</u> for most people.

So why are people so poor?

How can a person in today's wealthy environment with 40+ years of productive work, still end up relying on charity or government in retirement? How can people be so stupid, lazy or ignorant?

These are strong words but let us appreciate that experts predict that most people will live for an average of 20 years in retirement thus most people will live for 20 years in poverty!

The reason is simple. People do not plan to be to poor. They just did not plan to be financially secure either. They adopt the ostrich 'head in the sand' approach to financial planning hoping that they will win the lottery, inherit big cash or their children will make it rich (and look after them). Thus they fail to plan (and, therefore, plan to fail).

Bad Attitude

Many people also think they do not know where to find another plan to make money to create financial security or believe that they can make money. To cover up their ignorance they perpetuate the attitudes that *'you shouldn't talk about money'* or *'money is the root of all evil'*.

> ## The cost of these attitudes to money is stress and poverty

What is Financial Security?

'Financial Security' is having sufficient income producing assets to be able to live at your desired standard of living without having to work for money AND without relying on anyone else. You have personally 'secured' your financial future. You never have to work again, EVEN if you get a major illness and incur substantial medical costs.

Never-ending debt

Most people have a 'black belt' at spending money. Is that you?

If fact, most people are so good that they spend more money than they earn. Is that you?

How can we spend more than we earn? By borrowing, of course. Loans, credit cards, etc.

The startlingly news is that over 90% of people are now in debt and our debt levels have exploded over the past 20 years by 200-300% depending on the country and socio-economic group. So to create financial security in our lives, reduce stress and the threat of poverty in old age, not only do people have to invest for their future, they have to get out of debt as well.

Excess income is the key

The income you earn can be spent on either your lifestyle (for today) or your wealth (for tomorrow). If your income does not equal your lifestyle then you are going into debt and to poverty.

If your income equals your lifestyle then you are 'living for today' and thus you are not building wealth so have decided to feel financial stress today and to be poor in old age.

The only way to reduce financial stress and secure your future is to spend less on your lifestyle than you earn and thus create EXCESS INCOME to invest in your wealth and financial future.

The key to building assets is excess income

You must then invest your excess income into ASSETS that produce income. Assets such as shares (which Americans call 'stocks'), bonds, real estate and managed funds. An interest bearing bank account is not a sensible asset as it rarely produces a return that even keeps up with inflation.

> ### The Key to Financial Security is building a base of Income producing assets

Save or Invest?

Most people think they should be 'saving' for their future. This term is incorrect as it indicates the concept of storing money away. With the rising costs of living and longer lives, 'storing money' is not good enough, you need to be 'growing money'; that is 'investing'. This is why bank accounts are a waste of time.

How much should I invest?

The classic financial book, The Richest Man in Babylon, suggests that you should invest at **least 30% of your income**. Robert Kiyosaki in his classic book 'Rich Dad, Poor Dad' agrees with this figure.

Actually, you should be more sophisticated than this and you should get financial advice on how much you need to invest over what period of time to achieve your financial goals. Most people would be shocked by the amount they actually need to invest.

HOW DO YOU FEEL?

Most people will have read the previous paragraphs and feel absolutely nothing. This is because they will have convinced themselves that either their company or a government pension will look after them (delusion) or that they can never create excess income and if they did they would not know how to invest (ignorance). These attitudes guarantee stress, illness and poverty.

FACTS:

- Most pensions will not produce sufficient income for financial security, they are called 'under-funded' for good reason.
- Everyone can gain excellent advice to help them invest their money
- Everyone can create excess income to enable them to invest

How everyone can create excess income

Kiyosaki, in his book Cashflow Quadrant, explains that there are four ways to make money. Two are Active (left side) meaning you must be actively working or the money stops. These are employee and self-employed. On the other side of the quadrant are the 'passive' forms of earning an income; Investor or Business Owner. Passive means that they produce an income without your involvement.

Business Owners create 'systems' that make money even when they are not there. McDonalds is a great example of a business system that makes money. The success of McDonalds is not the hamburgers; it is the system that delivers the hamburgers. Investors own assets that produce income, in other words, their money makes money for them.

	Employee	Business Owner	
ACTIVE	———————————	———————————	PASSIVE
	Self-employed	Investor	

CASHFLOW QUADRANT™

An Employee works for someone else for a wage. The Self-employed person works on his own behalf and that is their main source of their income, such as accountants, retail shopkeepers, real estate agents, artists, plumbers, sportsmen and hair dressers. They 'own a job'.

The problem with both of these forms of 'active' income is if you stop working, you stop earning. The only way to overcome this dilemma is to earn excess income to invest in assets or build a business. Most people find it nearly impossible to generate sufficient excess income to achieve financial security and so must consider other ways of creating income. They must find ways of moving their earnings from the left-hand side of the quadrant to the right hand side.

The Network Marketing Solution

A Network Marketing network is based on working a 'people franchise' system. You work the system and thus you create an asset that will generate income. Eventually, it can generate income even without you working. Thus it moves from a self-employed ACTIVE income to a Business Owner passive income.

A Network Marketing opportunity's is a 'CASHFLOW CREATOR'; creating the cashflow you need to become financially secure, to drop all financial stresses in your life and live the way you choose. The new Network Marketing opportunity means that everyone can avoid poverty and achieve financial security.

*Cashflow Quadrant is a registered trademark of Cashflow Technologies Inc

ABOUT Ed Ludbrook

100% Leadership

Ed has a unique role in the Network Marketing industry as its Leadership expert and futurist. He is Europe's leading author and speaker who has sold over 2 million books in 20 languages.

As a futurist, Ed travels extensively speaking at conferences on the future of Direct Sales/Network Marketing. He is the Chairman of the Institute of Direct Sales Research and wrote the world's best-selling book on the future of Network Marketing.

To hire Ed as the keynote speaker at your next conference, email his office on admin@ludbrook.com

Ed has pioneered competence based Network Learning Systems in numerous teams around the world. Chairman of 100% Success Institute, global network learning company – see www.100percentinstitute.com

Raised in New Zealand, Edward graduated from Royal Military College Duntroon, Australia's prestigious army officer university. He served in the NZ Army Engineers then moved to London where he worked in investment banking and strategic consultancy before focusing on the Network Marketing industry.

When the industry has embraced his 100% vision based on the core concepts of competence based learning and leadership he intends to retire, help save the planet from global warming and produce a fantastic Rosé wine to celebrate life with his family in the sun.

GET The Knowledge™

The Knowledge is Network Marketing's first interactive elearning course designed to provide the new Networker with the Basic Theory everyone must learn to GUARANTEE their SUCCESS.

From the convenience of your own home, you can access SECRET **Knowledge** to:

- **Build your confidence to take massive action**
- **Achieve Maximum motivation**
- **Discover how to avoid the Gaps, Dips and Traps why 95% fail**
- **Learn the three key Network skills to Mastery**
- **Be able to coach anyone you sponsor to success**
- **Create momentum to become a leader**

This is the only course that will give you the confidence to sponsor anyone and KNOW they will succeed.

If you want to build a network based on a competence approach to networking the Knowledge will teach you how is the simplest and most fun way. This is interactive learning with multi-media coaching and quizzes to test your learning. On completion you will be certified by the 100% Success Institute.

The Knowledge will work with every Network System and will dramatically increase your results. For many people, it will be the difference between success and failure.

Go to www.100percentknowledge.com

100% Confidence CD

This is a summary of the 100% Confidence book that is very effective to provide a simple quick explanation of why someone should get involved with Network Marketing right now. Excellent for recruiting or in business kits to inspire all new networkers.

100% Success Basics

A quick and simple guide to Guaranteed Success in Network Marketing

This is the Basics book for the Competence boom in Network Marketing.
You will learn:
- How everyone can succeed
- How to create confidence and competence
- The only way you can become a leaders
- The three keys to a massive residual income

This will explain WHAT everyone needs to do to guarantee their success in network marketing. it will inspire them to act, inspire them to learn. It should be the first book everyone should read.

Published under the banner of the 100% Success Institute it is a completely generic title that everyone can use to educate new people. It works with every network system to provide the strategy for success.

100% Success Coach

Learning the skill that creates 100% Success

The only way to create competence is through effective coaching. Not performance coaching, competence coaching. They are different and the skill process is specific to Network Marketing.

Based on 12 years of trial and error within organisations around the world, this book is the bible on coaching and thus success in Network Marketing. IT explains WHAT and HOW to coach in all situations with all sorts of Networkers and Retailers. This includes, telephone, international and difficult person coaching. It includes how to run home workshops. It works will all programmes and systems.